5·56

NEW STEPS IN
RELIGIOUS
EDUCATION

This book is to be returned on or before
the last date stamped below.

WITHDRAWN

20,809   R00886   291 KEE

FRANCIS HOLLAND SCHOOL LIBRARY
CLARENCE GATE, LONDON NW1 6XR

LIBREX

D0183365

New Steps in Religious Education
Other books in the series

Book 1
1 This thing called religion
2 Sent by God
3 Jesus of Nazareth
4 Inside religious buildings
5 People at prayer
6 Feasts and festivals
7 Christian festivals

Book 3
1 One Church and many churches
2 God and the gods
3 Around birth
4 Growing up
5 Tying the knot
6 Death and beyond

Note: Throughout the series BCE (Before common or Christian era) and CE (common or Christian era) have been used in place of the traditional BC and AD.

Text © Michael Keene 1991

Original line illustrations © Stanley Thornes (Publishers) Ltd 1991

All rights reserved. No part of this publication may be reproduced or transmitted in any form or by any means, electronic or mechanical, including photocopy, recording, or any information storage and retrieval system, without permission in writing from the publisher or under licence from the Copyright Licensing Agency Limited. Further details of such licences (for reprographic reproduction) may be obtained from the Copyright Licensing Agency Limited, of 90, Tottenham Court Road, London W1P 9HE.

First published in 1991 by:
Stanley Thornes (Publishers) Ltd
Old Station Drive
Leckhampton
CHELTENHAM GL53 0DN
England

291 KEE
20,809

FRANCIS HOLLAND
SCHOOL LIBRARY

British Library Cataloguing in Publication Data
Keene, Michael
    New steps in religious education.
    Bk. 2
    1. Religions
    I. Title
    291

ISBN 1-871402-38-7

The cover pictures show the Ka'ba, Makka (© Camera Press), the Diwali Festival (© Hutchison Library), Putting Guru Granth Sahib to Bed Ceremony (© Judy Harrison), the Wailing Wall, Jerusalem (© Robert Harding), Saints Matthew and Mark (© British Museum).

Typeset in 11/13 Melior and Avant Garde by Tech-Set, Gateshead, Tyne & Wear
Printed and bound in Hong Kong.

Acknowledgements

The author and publishers would like to thank those members of the Christian, Jewish, Muslim, Hindu and Sikh communities who have advised and helped in the preparation of this book.

The publishers are grateful for permission to use copyright material, as follows:

The scripture quotations, unless otherwise indicated, are taken from the Holy Bible, New International Version, copyright © 1973, 1978, 1984 by International Bible Society, used by permission of Hodder & Stoughton Limited.

Quotations and illustrations from the Good News Bible, published by the Bible Societies/Collins. Old Testament © American Bible Society, New York 1976. Deuterocanonicals: © American Society 1979. New Testament: © American Bible Society, New York 1966, 1971 and 4th Edition 1976. Used by permission.
BBC for the quotation from *Worlds of Faith*, p. 73.
Pan Books for the extract from *Slowly Down the Ganges* by Eric Newby, p. 91.

Also the following for permission to reproduce copyright photographs and illustrations:

J.C. Allen, p. 11; Andes Press Agency/Carlos Reyes, p. 56; Bibliotheque Nationale, Paris, p. 10; British and Foreign Bible Society, p. 43; British Library, pp. 28(A), 38(A); Camera Press, pp. 18(A), 81(C), 84 (A and B), 86(A), 88(B); Coventry City Council, p. 86(B); Keith Ellis, pp. 58, 70 (C and D); Mary Evans Picture Library, p. 64(A); Format, pp. 32(B), 50, 67(C), 74(A), 78, 79(C) (Judy Harrison): 54 (Maggie Murray); Greenbelt p. 21; Sally and Richard Greenhill, pp. 28(B), 51, 66(A); Robert Harding, pp. 40(A), 53, 68(B), 70(B), 74(C), 82, 83, 87 (C and D); Geoff Howard, p. 61(B); Hutchison Library, pp. 8(B), 32(A), 52(A), 72(B), 79(B): 25, 46, 72 (A and C), 77 (Liba Taylor); London City Mission/Peter Trainer, p. 20(A); Mansell Collection, pp. 13, 14; Network, pp. 23, 48; Barry Page, p. 68(A); Ann and Bury Peerless, pp. 17, 30, 36(C), 66(B), 74(B), 76, 80(A), 90, 91, 92; Popperfoto, pp. 80(B), 88(A); Zev Radovan, pp. 26(A), 69; David Richardson, p. 24; Salvation Army, p. 20(B); Syndication International p. 38(B); Simon Warner, p. 55; Wycliffe Bible Translators, p. 42(B).

Contents

Unit 1 Christianity — then and now

Unit 2 The holy books

Unit 3 The Bible

Contents

Unit 4 Religious worship

Unit 5 Christian worship

Unit 6 Prophets, saints and gurus

Unit 7 Symbols in religion

Contents

Unit 8 Travelling

Words to remember

Unit 1 Christianity — then and now

1.1 A recap — how did it all begin?

Jesus was a Jew who lived nearly two thousand years ago in the tiny land of Palestine, a country in the Middle East which is now called Israel (map **A**). In area Palestine was about the same size as Wales. For a long time this country was under Roman control and, when Jesus was born, was ruled over by a puppet king of the Romans, Herod the Great.

The name 'Jesus' can be translated 'Joshua' and means 'God saves'. His second name, 'Christ' means 'anointed' as does another title applied to Jesus by his followers — the **Messiah.** In those days leaders, especially kings, had drops of precious oil sprinkled over their heads to show that God had set them apart for a special task. This was called 'anointing'. At the time of Jesus the Jewish people were waiting for God to send them a special Messiah who would expel the Romans from Palestine and give the Jews their freedom. For a time many Jews hoped that Jesus would be this warrior-leader.

Yet Jesus was neither a warrior nor an earthly king. He grew up in an ordinary family and sought to influence the people by his example and the power of his preaching. For a long time there were few who really believed his message. Then his followers became gradually convinced that God had put his own son on earth to show the people just how God expected them to behave.

For three years Jesus travelled around Palestine with his twelve disciples, who were chosen by him to continue his work after he had left the earth. The Gospels tell us that during this time Jesus spent a great deal of time arguing with the Jewish religious leaders, caring for the poor and sick, performing many miracles and teaching the people by **parables** or stories.

Jesus built up a large following amongst the people and this disturbed the religious authorities who came to believe that Jesus and his followers were becoming too powerful. They wanted Jesus dead. Eventually **Pontius Pilate,** the Roman governor, was persuaded to sign his death warrant. Pilate accepted that Jesus was a threat to the Roman Empire. It was in about 29 CE that Jesus was put to death.

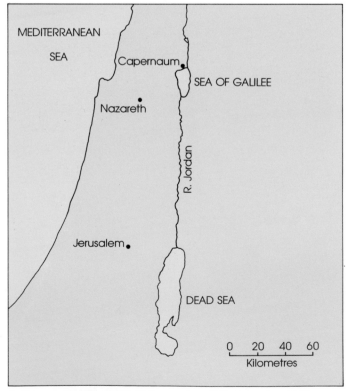

A The country into which Jesus was born. What was it called?

B 'I saw the Spirit come down like a dove.' (John 1.32)

Three days later, according to the Gospels, Jesus came back from the dead (the **resurrection**). After another 40 days he left the earth altogether. Before doing so, however, he told his disciples that they must preach God's message throughout the world. They were so successful in doing this that by the fourth century the Roman Empire was ruled by a Christian emperor.

C 'He will go and look for the lost sheep.' (Matthew 18.12)

Words to remember

The **Messiah** was God's anointed leader who, the Jews believed, would deliver them from Roman domination.

A **parable** is a story told to make people think about a religious lesson or moral.

Pontius Pilate was the Roman governor of Judaea from 26–36 CE. He later fell into disgrace and there is a tradition which says that he committed suicide.

The most important Christian belief of all is that, three days after he died, Jesus Christ came back from the dead. This is known as the **resurrection.**

A key question

Why did the opponents of Jesus want him put to death?

Do you know...

▶ in which country Jesus lived and who controlled it at the time?

▶ which special leader the Jews were waiting for when Jesus was born?

▶ how long Jesus travelled through Palestine and what he did during this time?

▶ what happened at the end of Jesus' life on earth?

Things to do

1 Write a sentence to answer each of these questions:
   a What does the name 'Jesus' mean?
   b What do the titles 'Christ' and 'Messiah' mean?
   c Why did Jesus choose twelve disciples?
   d What is a parable?
   e What do Christians believe happened to Jesus after he was put to death?

2 The *Good News Bible* is a modern translation of the Bible. It contains some very unusual drawings. You can see two of them in **B** and **C**. They are of incidents in the life of Jesus. Copy them into your book and underneath each write a brief description of what it illustrates. Use the Bible references to help you.

3 In this extract St Paul is trying to describe to some young Christians in the city of Philippi what Jesus did:

   ⁶Who, being in very nature God . . .
   . . . made himself nothing, taking the very nature of a servant, being made in human likeness.
   ⁸And being found in appearance as a man, he humbled himself and became obedient to death – even death on a cross!

   Use the text on the opposite page to help you answer each of these questions:
   a What did Jesus' followers believe was the purpose of him appearing on earth in 'human likeness'?
   b St Paul says that Jesus 'became obedient to death'. What did Jesus do during his time on earth?
   c Write your own summary of the life of Christ in not more than 50 words.

1.2 The Day of Pentecost

After the four Gospels in the New Testament comes the **Acts of the Apostles.** This book was written round about 75 CE by a disciple of Jesus called **Luke.** He also wrote the Gospel which carries his name and it seems likely that Luke's Gospel and the Acts of the Apostles were originally one single book.

Most of what we know about the beginning and early years of the Christian Church we learn from the Acts of the Apostles. In the blue box you can read Luke's description of the events that led to the formation of the Christian Church. Notice several things about the story:

▶ the disciples were huddled together and frightened that the persecution which had claimed the life of Jesus would soon affect them as well. In fact, for the time being, it did not.
▶ the **Holy Spirit** invaded their gathering and what happened next can only be described in picture form.

> ²Suddenly a sound like the blowing of a violent wind came from heaven and filled the whole house where they were sitting. ³They saw what seemed to be tongues of fire that separated and came to rest on each of them.

▶ those who were present began to speak in strange languages or 'tongues'.

The reason for the tongues soon became apparent as we are told that people from many different countries had gathered in the city of Jerusalem at this time. They had come for the very important Jewish festival of **Pentecost (A).** The disciples were able to preach to them in their own languages. You can see from map **B** where many of these people came from.

A What does the Jewish festival of Pentecost commemorate?

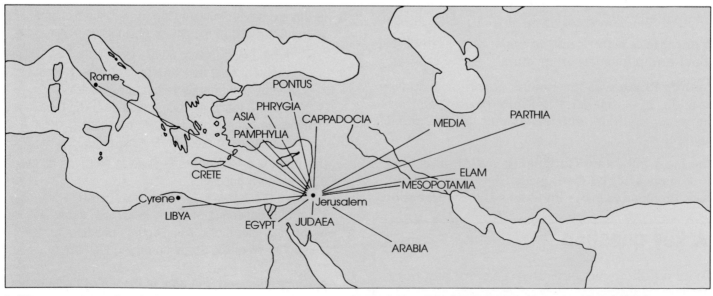

B Why were so many Jews in Jerusalem at this time and what impact did the events of the Day of Pentecost have on many of them?

Those people who listened to the disciples speaking in their own language returned home when the festival finished. Amongst them were many who believed the message that the disciples preached to them. Already the Christian message had begun to spread beyond the city of Jerusalem and into the further reaches of the Roman Empire.

Christians do not agree amongst themselves as to just what happened on the Day of Pentecost. There are those who think that the event took place just as it is described by Luke. Others insist that Luke was simply using symbols (fire and wind) to try to convey something of the excitement and bewilderment of what actually happened. Most would agree, however, that here we have the birth of the Christian Church.

Words to remember

The **Acts of the Apostles** tells the story of the Christian Church from the resurrection of Jesus through to the imprisonment of Paul in Rome.

In the Bible the **Holy Spirit** is the third person of the Christian Trinity after God the Father and God the Son.

As far as we know **Luke,** the author of Acts, was a doctor who accompanied Paul on some of his missionary journeys.

Pentecost is the Jewish festival commemorating the giving of the Ten Commandments on Mount Sinai, which follows fifty days after the Festival of Passover.

Do you know...

▶ how Luke describes the excitement and bewilderment brought about by the giving of the Holy Spirit?
▶ why this event was the most important in the history of the Christian Church?

A key question

Why do Christians regard the Day of Pentecost as marking the birth of the Christian Church?

Acts of the Apostles 2.1-6

When the day of Pentecost came, they were all together in one place. [2]Suddenly a sound like the blowing of a violent wind came from heaven and filled the whole house where they were sitting. [3]They saw what seemed to be tongues of fire that separated and came to rest on each of them. [4]All of them were filled with the Holy Spirit and began to speak in other tongues as the Spirit enabled them.

[5]Now there were staying in Jerusalem God-fearing Jews from every nation under heaven. [6]When they heard this sound, a crowd came together in bewilderment, because each one heard them speaking in his own language.

▶ Read this extract carefully. Does it strike you as a description of something that actually took place or a symbolic description of that event?

Things to do

1 Answer each of these questions in your own words using the information on the opposite page:
   a Who wrote the Acts of the Apostles and what is the link between the fifth book of the New Testament and one of the Gospels?
   b Why is the Acts of the Apostles a very important book to the Christian Church?
   c Why were all of the disciples of Jesus and other followers huddled together in a single house?
   d Why would many of the people who had come to Jerusalem for the Festival of Pentecost have cause to remember this particular year?

2 Copy map **B** into your books. Can you find the modern names for three of the countries shown on this map?

3 Imagine that you were an early Christian disciple who was shattered and disillusioned after the death of Jesus. Describe the impact that the resurrection of Jesus followed by the giving of the Holy Spirit on the Day of Pentecost might have had upon you.

1.3 Peter and Paul

Peter was born in the small fishing port of Bethsaida, on the shores of Lake Galilee. His fisherman father, John, named him Simon but Jesus nicknamed him Peter from the Greek word meaning 'rock'. This nickname was to assume considerable importance for whole generations of later Christians.

No disciple of Jesus is more prominent in the Gospels than Peter. The picture that we have of him is, above all, that of a rash and hot-blooded man who is always opening his mouth before he has really thought out what he wants to say. Yet, even when he did so, he seemed to see and recognise things that the other disciples did not notice. He was, for instance, the first to recognise Jesus as God's Messiah. He stated that he was prepared to lay down his life for this Messiah and yet, days later, was to be found denying three times that he ever knew him. After the death of Jesus, though, Peter was one of the first to meet the risen Jesus and he became the first recognised leader of the Early Church.

A According to tradition, how were Peter and Paul put to death?

Some people believe that Peter became the first Bishop of Rome, although there is no evidence for this. Roman Catholics believe that the **Pope,** as the Bishop of Rome, is St Peter's successor. Other churches do not accept this. We are not sure how Peter died but he was probably crucified by Emperor Nero in 64 CE.

There is a tradition [**A**] that Peter was crucified upside down because he did not consider himself worthy to die in the same way as Jesus had died.

Paul was originally a strict **Pharisee,** a Roman citizen and an early persecutor of the Christian Church. He travelled from Damascus in order to oppose the Christians, underwent a dramatic conversion and, according to the New Testament, became one of the disciples of Jesus that he had been persecuting. You can read about this conversion in the blue box.

After he became a Christian Paul dedicated the rest of his life to travelling throughout the Roman Empire, preaching about Jesus. During these travels many dramatic things happened to him:

▶ he had a violent disagreement with Peter over whether non-Jews had to accept Jewish religious traditions when they became Christians.
▶ he was put into prison and flogged.
▶ he was seized by a mob and almost lynched before Roman soldiers intervened.
▶ he was shipwrecked on his way to Rome to stand trial.

We are not too sure how Paul died but it is likely that he was beheaded in the same persecution in which Peter died.

Do you know...

▶ what Peter's first name was and why it was changed by Jesus?
▶ who is thought by many to be the modern successor of Peter?
▶ how Paul became a Christian?

B This photograph shows the Straight Street in Damascus — but why did Paul end up there?

Acts 9.3-9

³As he neared Damascus on his journey, suddenly a light from heaven flashed around him. ⁴He fell to the ground and heard a voice say to him, "Saul, Saul, why do you persecute me?"

⁵"Who are you, Lord?" Saul asked.

"I am Jesus, whom you are persecuting," he replied. ⁶"Now get up and go into the city, and you will be told what you must do."

⁷The men travelling with Saul stood there speechless; they heard the sound but did not see anyone. ⁸Saul got up from the ground, but when he opened his eyes he could see nothing. So they led him by the hand into Damascus. ⁹For three days he was blind, and did not eat or drink anything.

Words to remember

Paul was a zealous Jew who set out to destroy the Christian Church but, after a dramatic conversion, was to become its most important leader.

Peter was a disciple of Jesus, an early Church leader and was, according to tradition, crucified in Rome.

The **Pharisees** were a very strict Jewish sect who frequently came into conflict with Jesus.

The **Pope** is the head of the Roman Catholic Church who lives in the Vatican in Rome.

A key question

Why were Peter and Paul so important in the early Christian Church?

Things to do

1 **B** shows the street in Damascus, Straight Street, on which Paul is thought to have been converted. Imagine that you are a local radio reporter sent to cover this dramatic event. Make a tape recording describing the scene soon after the event. Carry out an interview or two with the people who were travelling with Paul — and with the great man himself. Try to find out as much as you can about what might have happened.

2 Copy and complete these sentences using the words listed below. Just to make things a little more difficult the letters in each word have been jumbled up.
   a The Roman emperor believed to have executed Peter and Paul was _____.
   b Roman Catholics believe that Peter was the first _____ of Rome.
   c Before he became a Christian Paul was a strict _____.
   d Paul was converted to Christianity on his way to the city of _____.

   eoNr   spBohi   iParhese   uDmcasas

3 Compare and contrast the characters and lives of Peter and Paul.

1.4 Christianity in the Roman Empire

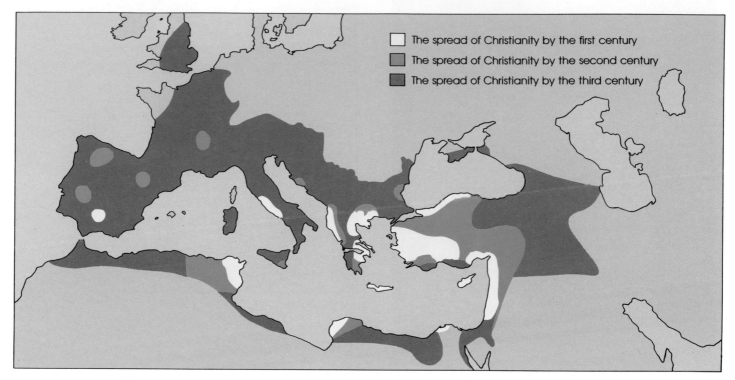

A The way in which Christianity spread through the Roman Empire between the first and the third centuries.

Peter and Paul were not the only Christian missionaries in the Early Church. Apart from the known disciples such as Thomas, who is believed to have preached in India, hundreds of unknown believers talked about their faith wherever they went. You can see how rapidly the Christian faith spread by looking at map **A.**

From time to time some of the Roman emperors did try to wipe out the Christian religion, believing it to be a threat to the Empire. **Nero** was one such emperor. According to Tacitus, a Roman historian, Nero tried to blame the Christians for a fire that he himself had started in Rome. He rounded up hundreds of Christians and set fire to them. No one knows just how many Christians died at his hands. Nor do we know how many died at the hands of other Roman emperors. However, we do know that many Christians were thrown to the lions in the Colosseum in Rome, the famous amphitheatre where gladiatorial fights were held.

Then, at the beginning of the fourth century, **Constantine** was involved in a bitter battle with Maxentius over who should become the emperor. Alarmed by reports that Maxentius was using magic to defeat him, Constantine prayed to the 'Supreme God' for help. The response was a sign, a cross in the noon-day sky 'above the sun' with the words 'Conquer by this'. That night, Constantine claimed, Christ appeared to him in a dream and told him to use the sign of the cross at the head of his army as a safeguard in all his engagements with his enemies.

Constantine obeyed, miraculously his armies won and the Christian religion was officially recognised throughout the Roman Empire. The days of persecution for the Christians at the hands of the Romans were now over. Yet the victory was short-lived. The Roman Empire was already showing signs of crumbling. Within less than a century its armies had withdrawn from most parts of the Empire, shortly to disappear for ever.

B Why has Nero gone down in history as the cruellest of all the Roman emperors?

Words to remember

Constantine came to power in 312 CE and was the first Roman Emperor to accept the Christian message.

Nero was the Roman Emperor from 54–68 CE who acted with great cruelty towards the Christian Church.

A key question

Why did Constantine become a Christian and how did it change the way that he ran his Empire?

Do you know...

► why some Roman emperors tried to wipe out the Christian religion?
► who blamed the Christians for a fire that he himself started in Rome?
► who the first Christian emperor was and what difference it made to the Christian Church?

Things to do

1   **B** shows the Roman Emperor Nero. Tacitus describes for us how Nero treated the Christians that he arrested:

> First those who confessed to being Christians were arrested. Then, on information obtained from them, hundreds were convicted, more for their anti-social beliefs than for fire-raising. In their deaths they were made a mockery. They were covered in the skins of wild animals, torn to death by dogs, crucified or set on fire — so that when darkness fell they burned like torches in the night. Nero opened up his own gardens for this spectacle and gave a show in the arena, where he mixed with the crowd, or stood dressed as a charioteer on a chariot.

   a   Explain, by using the information on the opposite page, the reference here to 'fire-raising'.
   b   Using what you have read about Nero to help you, explain in your own words what type of person you think he was.

2   Imagine that you are a Christian in the days of Emperor Nero. For days now he has been rounding up your Christian friends and putting them cruelly to death. Keep a diary recording your thoughts and actions as you expect the Roman soldiers to arrive and arrest you at any time.

3   Tertullian was a Christian writer who lived through much of the Roman persecution. In this extract he tries to explain why the early Christians were singled out for such harsh treatment:

> If the River Tiber reaches the walls, if the River Nile does not rise to the fields, if the sky does not move or the earth does, if there is a famine, if there is a plague, the cry is at once 'The Christians to the lions'. What, all of them to one lion?

   a   Why do you think that each of the natural disasters mentioned in this quotation was blamed on the early Christians?
   b   What is Tertullian trying to say when he asks 'What, all of them to one lion?'
   c   Look in a dictionary to discover what a 'scapegoat' is. Do you think that this word accurately describes the position of the Christians in the Roman Empire?

1.5 Christianity arrives in Britain

No one is quite sure how, or when, the Christian message first arrived in Britain. Probably a good number of the Roman soldiers who settled in Britain were Christians. The story of Christianity in those early days, however, is usually associated with the work of a handful of people.

St Ninian has been described as 'the first and the greatest of the ancient Christian missionaries', yet we know next to nothing about him. It does seem, however, that he established a monastery at Whithorn in Scotland.

A What does St Patrick appear to be doing in this drawing?

Fortunately rather more is known about **St Patrick** (389–461 CE). He was kidnapped at the age of sixteen while staying on his father's farm in the west of Britain and was taken as a slave to Ireland. During the six years of slavery that followed his own faith in God deepened considerably. Until this time religion had meant little but now, as a slave of heathen masters who had no faith in God, his own prayers became very real to him.

> Day by day as I went, a shepherd with my flock, I used to pray constantly . . . a hundred prayers a day, and nearly as many at night, staying out in the woods or on the mountain. And before daybreak I was up for prayer, in snow or frost or rain.

At the end of six years of slavery a voice in a dream told Patrick 'your ship is ready'. He managed to escape from slavery and walked two hundred miles to the nearest port. He arrived back in England only to hear the voice of the Irish people calling out to him:

> We beseech you to come and walk among us once more.

So, in 432 CE, Patrick returned to spend the last thirty years of his life working in Ireland. Although not well-educated himself he encouraged learning and the building of many monasteries. Also, as you can see from **A,** many miracles were attached to his name. In this engraving he is banishing frogs and other troublesome vermin into the marshes.

Ireland was the birth-place of **St Columba** (521–597 CE) who became a famous abbot and missionary. In 563 CE, along with twelve friends, he set out from Irish shores to undertake a 'pilgrimage for Christ'. The pilgrimage took him to **Iona** on the west coast of Scotland. Here he established a monastery and started to preach to people who knew nothing about the Christian faith. Iona was to remain Columba's headquarters for thirty-four years whilst he and his followers converted a large part of Scotland to Christianity.

The Life of St Columba

Most of our information about Columba comes from *The Life of St Columba*, written by Adamnan, Abbot of Iona from 679 to 704 CE. Here are some extracts:

> From boyhood he had given himself as a Christian recruit to studies in quest of wisdom . . . God bestowed upon him a sound body and a pure mind . . . he was angelic in appearance, bright in speech, holy in deeds, excellent in gifts and great in counsel. He could not let an hour go past without applying himself to prayer, reading, writing or some sort of work . . . he was dear to everybody, always showing a cheerful, holy face.

▶ Explain in your own words what you think each of these phrases means:
  a '. . . a sound body and a pure mind'.
  b '. . . he was angelic in appearance, bright in speech, holy in deeds, excellent in gifts and great in counsel.'

▶ Imagine that Columba has just died. Write an obituary (a summary of someone's life, character and achievements, which is written after their death) for a newspaper. Use the information that you are given above and on the opposite page.

Words to remember

St Columba was the famous abbot and missionary who established a religious community on the island of Iona.

Iona is a small island in the Inner Hebrides, off Scotland, where St Columba founded a monastery in 563 CE.

St Ninian was a very early Christian missionary in Britain about whom little is known.

It was **St Patrick** who took the Christian message to the Irish.

A key question

Who were the earliest Christian missionaries to the British Isles and what motivated them in their work?

Do you know...

▶ how the Christian religion probably first arrived in Britain?
▶ why St Patrick ended up taking the Christian message to the Irish?
▶ which famous religious community was founded by St Columba?

Things to do

1 Write out and complete the following sentences:
  a _____ was the 'first and the greatest of the ancient British missionaries'.
  b _____ was the great missionary to the Irish.
  c _____ took the Christian message from Ireland across to the Island of Iona.
  d St Patrick encouraged _____ and the building of _____.

2 An Irish legend describes how a witch threw garlic water at Patrick as part of a spell to kill him. The saint, however, promptly threw back a hand-ball (which missionaries carried) and this killed the witch on the spot. After the angels comforted him St Patrick is believed to have prayed that Ireland would never lose its Christian faith.
  a Miraculous stories often become attached to saints. Can you think of any reason why this story should have been attached to St Patrick?
  b Why do you think that miraculous stories such as this one grew up in the first place?
  c Do you know of any other legends which are told about saints — possibly St Patrick? Tell each other your stories. Choose the most interesting ones and divide into groups. Each group should then write up one story, using your own words, and draw pictures to illustrate it. Put all the stories and illustrations together to make a wall display.

Christianity — then and now

1.6 'Angels not Angles'

A In this painting, why is Augustine preaching to King Ethelbert and Queen Bertha?

According to tradition **Gregory,** a monk in Rome, saw some attractive children in the town's market. On asking about them he discovered that they were 'Anglii' (from England) and that they were 'pagans' (heathens, having no Christian beliefs). His famous reply was that the children were 'Angels and not Angles'.

In 596 CE Gregory, now Pope, sent a team of forty monks under **Augustine** to England. When they landed, Augustine sent a message to King Ethelbert telling him that they had come from Rome

> ... bringing good news of everlasting joy in heaven and a kingdom that knows no end, with the true and living God.

The king told them to stay where they were until he had decided what to do with them.

In the end he allowed them to stay. Within a few months the King had followed his Queen in becoming a Christian (**A**). He gave the monks a palace in Canterbury and allowed them to preach freely. Today Canterbury Cathedral (**B**) is still the mother church of **Anglicans** in England.

Pope Gregory sent a message to Augustine advising him that the English should be brought slowly away from belief in their old gods towards the Christian faith. There were in fact many Christians in England already but they did not take too kindly to the preaching of Augustine. For almost a century these two groups of Christians had little to do with each other.

There is no denying the success of Augustine's work. A large number of English people became Christians. The **Venerable Bede** tells us:

> Then greater numbers began to come together to hear the word and to forsake their heathen ways and join the church. The King was known to be pleased at their faith and conversion, not that he would drive anyone to the Christian fold, for those who prepared him for baptism had taught him that one must choose to serve Christ, not be forced to it.

A key question

How important was the work of St Augustine in converting the English to Christianity?

B Which cathedral is the mother church of all Anglicans and why?

A hermit's advice

Here Bede informs us of the advice given by a hermit (a solitary monk) to British bishops at a conference organised by Augustine.

If he is a man of God, follow him. How shall we know? Our Lord said 'I am meek and lowly of heart'. If he is meek and lowly he may bear the yoke of Christ. But how shall we know? Let him arrive first. When you come in, if he rise up and greet you, hear him submissively. If not, he despises you and I say, despise you him.

▶ There is one part of this advice which is surprising, coming, as it does, from one Christian to other Christians. What is it?
▶ Why is it surprising?

Words to remember

An **Anglican** is a person who is a member of the Church of England.

Augustine was sent by Pope Gregory as a missionary to England. He became the first Archbishop of Canterbury in 597 CE.

Gregory was a Benedictine monk who built many monasteries and was elected Pope in 590 CE.

The **Venerable Bede** was a famous monk, scholar and writer who lived from 673 to 735 CE.

Do you know...

▶ why Pope Gregory sent Augustine to convert the English?
▶ where Augustine set up his headquarters?
▶ what position Augustine occupied after preaching to the English?

Things to do

1 Copy out and complete the following crossword.

Across
3 Having no Christian beliefs (7).
4 Leader of the team of monks sent to Britain by Pope Gregory (9).
5 This Pope advised bringing the English slowly to the Christian faith (7).
6 Augustine told King Ethelbert that he would find this in heaven (3).

Down
1 The mother church of Anglicans in England (10).
2 This monk was also a famous writer (4).

2 Explain, in your own words, how Augustine came to land in England and describe the work that he then did.

3 Look at **A.** What might Augustine be saying to King Ethelbert? What might King Ethelbert's reply be? Write down their conversation in the form of a scene from a play. Include other characters if you want to.

1.7 So many different churches

The Christian Church today is divided into many different groups or denominations. In fact, there are now thought to be over 20,000 different denominations throughout the world. Yet it was not always like this. To find out why the Church began to split up in this way we must look back into history.

The Christian religion started with a small group of followers of Jesus of Nazareth. Within a few years, however, it had spread through the whole Roman Empire and within three hundred years Christianity had become the official Roman religion. In the centuries that followed, the Christian religion reached Europe, then Australia and America. As it spread widely so it began to split up into many of the denominations that we have today. Each denomination preferred its own way of worshipping God and that is why there are still hundreds of different Christian groups.

It is very important to realise that we are talking about different 'branches' of the Christian Church and not different religions. Most of the branches which exist today fall into one of four broad groups:

▶ The **Roman Catholic Church.** The centre of this Church is in Vatican City which is a small, self-governing area in Rome. The Head of the Catholic Church is the Pope. The present Pope is John Paul II who was born in Poland and elected in 1978 (**A**). Today about sixty per cent of all Christians are Catholics.
▶ The **Orthodox Church.** Although this Church was originally based in Constantinople, most Orthodox Christians are now found in Russia and Greece.
▶ The **Protestant Church.** During the sixteenth century the Reformation took place in Europe. This was a protest against the corruption of the Catholic Church. In England the **Church of England** was formed by Henry VIII as a part of this protest.
▶ The **Nonconformist churches.** Between 1650 and 1900 some Christians wanted to carry their 'protest' further. They formed 'Nonconformist' churches, amongst which are the Baptists, the Methodists and the Salvation Army.

Since 1945 many Christians from different denominations have worked together increasingly. Although the official coming together of the main groups is still a long way off, individual Christians have been leading the way. They now have meetings together, pray together and celebrate Holy Communion with each other. This coming together is known as the **Ecumenical Movement.**

You will be finding out more about these churches, their individual ways of worship, their distinctive beliefs and the Ecumenical Movement in Book Three.

A Find out three things that Roman Catholics believe about the Pope.

SERVICES

- Hereford Cathedral: 8am, Holy Communion; 10am, The Cathedral Eucharist, Preacher: The Treasurer; 11.30am, Matins; 3.30pm, Evensong (attended by members of the medical profession), Preacher: The Rev. Canon John H. Brewer, Canon Emeritus of Accra. Tuesday: 1.05pm–1.30pm, Prayers for Peace.

- St Barnabas, Venns Lane: 10am, Parish Mass and Sunday School; 6.30pm, Evening Prayer.

- St Peter's: 8am, Holy Communion; 10.30am, Parish Communion; 6.30pm, Evening Worship.

- Holy Trinity: 10am, Parish Eucharist, Sunday School and Baptism; 6.30pm, Evensong and Sermon.

- St Paul's, Tupsley: 8am, Holy Communion; 9.30am, Family Service and Church Parade; 6.30pm, Parish Communion.

- Salvation Army, Canonmoor Street: 10.30am and 6pm, Belfast Temple, Northern Ireland, Home League Singers.

- Society of Friends (Quakers), King Street; 10.30am, Meeting for Worship and Children's Class.

- Elim Pentecostal Church, Clive Street: 9.45am, Sunday School; 11am, Communion, and Worship, Rev. Philip Thompsett; 6.30pm, Evening Praise, Mr Jonathan Priday.

- Jubilee Christian Centre, Preston-on-Wye: Main meetings in the Village Hall: 10.30am, Worship and Breaking of Bread; 11am, Junior Church; 6pm, Evening Celebration.

- Staunton-on-Wye Free Church: 3pm, Family Service.

- Marden Chapel: 6.30pm, Mr B. Pryce, of Hereford.

B Find a similar list of church services from your local paper and compare it with this list taken from a newspaper in Hereford.

A key question

Why have so many Christian churches sprung up in the last 2000 years?

Do you know...

▶ what a Christian denomination is?
▶ why the Christian Church split up into different denominations?
▶ what the main Christian denominations are?

Words to remember

The **Church of England** was first formed by King Henry VIII to act as the national church of this country.

The **Ecumenical Movement** is an attempt to bring together churches of all denominations.

Nonconformist churches are those which do not belong to the Anglican or Roman Catholic denominations.

The **Orthodox Church** is made up of Russian and Greek Orthodox Christians together with members of other, smaller Churches.

The **Protestant Church** was formed as a protest against the Roman Catholic Church in the sixteenth century.

The largest Christian denomination is the **Roman Catholic Church** whose head is the Pope.

Things to do

1 Answer these questions in complete sentences, using your own words.
   a How long did it take the Christian religion to become the official religion of the Roman Empire?
   b Which denomination has about sixty per cent of all Christians among its members?
   c Which Church now has the most members in Russia and Greece?
   d Under which king was the Church of England formed?

2 Here are five words or phrases which are used on the opposite page. Write two sentences about each of them to show that you understand what they mean.
   a Denomination
   b The Roman Catholic Church
   c The Eastern Orthodox Church
   d The Protestant Church
   e Nonconformist churches

3 Find out how many different denominations there are in the area or town in which you live. Take one of them which particularly interests you, visit the church and find out as much about it as you can.

Christianity — then and now

1.8 The teaching goes on

A What particular kinds of help do you think these people might need from this London City Missioner?

As the early Christian Church fanned out through the Roman Empire to spread the message of Jesus it set a pattern for future generations to follow. Pope Gregory did so when he sent Augustine and his fellow monks as missionaries to England in the sixth century. Much later, in 1792, William Carey, a Northamptonshire cobbler, trod in the same footsteps when he left this country to become a missionary in India.

Since the time of Carey, the first 'modern' missionary, countless other people have gone to work overseas as Christian missionaries. Others realised that their own country was a mission field and have worked amongst the poor and needy of Britain. The London City Mission, for example, was set up in 1835 to work amongst all those in need on the streets of the country's capital city. Today the LCM has 130 full-time and voluntary missioners active in London's markets, housing estates, shops, factories and theatres (**A**). There are now similar missions in other large cities such as Birmingham, Manchester and Glasgow.

More well-known was the work of William Booth and the Salvation Army, which started in 1865.

B This Salvation Army officer is bringing a welcome cup of tea to some firemen after a fire. Why do you think that the Salvation Army is involved in this kind of work?

The Salvation Army has become a familiar sight on the streets of most towns and cities. Over the years it has run mission halls (called citadels), soup-kitchens, hostels for the unemployed and a rescue agency for people who have left home. Both in this country and overseas the Salvation Army is quick to respond to homelessness, natural disasters and local and national emergencies (**B**).

Much of today's Christian activity goes on outside church buildings. Some novel ways have been found to communicate the Christian message. These include Christian coffee bars, beach missions during the summer months and large Christian arts and music festivals held in the open air. The largest of these festivals, Greenbelt, attracts 25,000 young people each year (**C**).

A key question

How have Christians communicated their message in recent years and how is this work continuing today?

C Is rock music an effective way of presenting the Christian message to young people?

Do you know...

▶ how the example of the early Christians in spreading the Christian message was followed by later generations of Christians?
▶ what kind of work the London City Mission and the Salvation Army do today?

Things to do

1 In **C** you can see one of the performers at Greenbelt, the largest Christian arts festival. Each year this arts festival draws thousands of Christian young people.
   a How would you expect a Christian arts festival to differ from an ordinary arts festival?
   b Do you think that this is a good way of interesting young people in the Christian religion?
   c Can you think of any drawbacks of this way of communicating the Christian message?

2 In December 1985 the Church of England appointed a vicar to find out why fewer and fewer people were going to church in inner-city areas. Imagine that you have just become the vicar of one such church in the centre of one of this country's largest cities. When you arrive to take up your appointment the average number in your congregation for a service is just twenty. How would you set about attracting people to come to your church? What types of event would you organise to try to attract people?

3 Find out all that you can about the work of the Salvation Army. In particular, try to find answers to the following questions:
   a Why do members of the Salvation Army wear their distinctive uniform and why is this organisation called an army?
   b What is it that attracts many people to the Salvation Army?
   c What is the Salvation Army doing in your area?
   d Try to find recent examples of disasters in which the Salvation Army was actively involved in bringing help and comfort.

Christianity — then and now

1.9 The Christian Church today

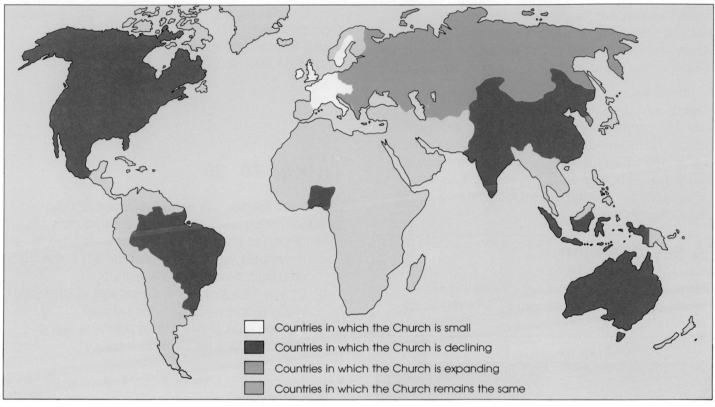

Key:
- Countries in which the Church is small
- Countries in which the Church is declining
- Countries in which the Church is expanding
- Countries in which the Church remains the same

A Using an atlas, can you list some countries in which the Christian Church is growing and some in which it is declining?

In some countries of the world today the Christian Church is growing very rapidly. In others, as you can see from **A,** church membership is declining.

In its early days Christianity established itself firmly in North Africa but, since the religion of Islam was born and flourished in that part of the world, the number of those converted to Christianity has been small. In most parts of North Africa the Christian Church is not allowed to 'evangelise' or make new converts. However, in other parts of Africa, most notably in Central and West Africa, the situation is very different. Today there are between 100 and 150 million Christians in this area alone. Many of the churches to which these Christians belong are independent. This means that they do not belong to the main Christian denominations. Centred very much upon the Bible, many of them carry out healing as part of their worship. The Ethiopian church is one which

offers dance as well as music as part of their worship of God.

In South and Central America too, many new churches have sprung up. These churches worship God in a way which makes their worshippers feel at home. Dancing, clapping, chanting and swaying are essential elements of church services in this part of the world, and the services can go on for hours. In this part of America many priests identify with the poor and needy in their community and lead the protests against those who exploit them.

In the USA church-going is much stronger than it is in this country. Whilst in Britain only one in ten adults go to church on any given Sunday, in America that figure is five times as high. An interesting feature of church-going in the USA is that Sunday schools are often not just for children but for all members of the family.

In many countries of the world Christians have total freedom to worship but in some countries that freedom is very restricted or non-existent. Until recently Christians were imprisoned for their religious beliefs in many Communist countries and some were even put to death. There are still some countries in which it remains illegal for a group of Christians to come together to worship.

A key question

Is the Church declining throughout the world or are there places where the number of Christians is on the increase?

B 'Our own church'. Why have many Christians who have come to this country to live formed their own churches?

Do you know...

▶ in which countries it is still illegal for the Christian church to worship or preach?
▶ what is unusual about the churches that have sprung up in West and Central Africa?
▶ why some churches are attracting more and more worshippers?

Things to do

1 A young African woman, aged 19, came to this country to study. As a Christian she had gone to the nearest church on her first Sunday here. Here are a few extracts from a letter she wrote to her mother describing how she felt.

> I felt very strange . . . the church was very large and cold . . . the hymns were accompanied by an organ and no one clapped or swayed . . . the sermon only lasted for about ten minutes and the congregation did not make a sound . . . the service was over within an hour . . . no one said how nice it was to see me or welcomed me at all . . . I will try another church next Sunday, maybe I was just unlucky.

a Although she does not say so in as many words, this woman is comparing worship in her own country and the church that she went to in Britain. What are the main differences that she notices?
b Many people from overseas who now live in this country have formed churches of their own. **B** shows you one such church. Why do you think that they have done this?

2 On 16th July 1972 Ivan Vasilievich Moiseyev died at the hands of the secret police in Russia. He was a soldier who refused to give up his faith in Christ. He was charged with:

> . . . infringing the rights of your fellow-soldiers in your unit and company and in other units with which you had contact. Your continuous observance (habit) of prayer and preaching are intolerable (unacceptable) to others around you . . .

to which Moiseyev replied:

> I have never harassed (pestered) others with the preaching of the Gospel. I don't consider it a crime to give bread to the hungry.

a Does it surprise you that in the twentieth century people are still being put to death for what they believe?
b Can you suggest reasons why the Church often grows most rapidly in countries in which its members are persecuted?
c Can you find another example of a modern church suffering persecution?

Unit 2 The holy books

2.1 Why are holy books so important?

Each religion has its own Holy Scriptures. Just what this means will become clear as we look at each religion in turn. In general terms, a Scripture is a book in which God's message has been written and which has been carefully preserved over a long period of time.

That period of time can be very long indeed. The Bible, for instance, took almost 1500 years to write, although the books in the New Testament were completed in less than a century. You will find out more about the Bible, the holy book for all Christians, in Unit 3. Most of the holy books, however, were completed much more quickly.

A The Guru Granth Sahib is carried above the heads of the worshippers. In which religious building is this happening?

Naturally, the followers of each religion believe that their own Scriptures are unique and have come directly from God. For this reason they are often called 'The Word of God'. To Muslims, for example, the **Qur'an** is the perfect record of the revelations which were given to the Prophet Muhammad by Allah. The Prophet taught these revelations to the people during his lifetime and his followers wrote them down.

In the light of this it is hardly surprising that worshippers treat their Scriptures with the greatest possible care and respect. You will discover this if you ever visit a Sikh temple (a gurdwara) where the **Guru Granth Sahib** is always carried above the heads of the worshippers to show its exalted position in their faith (**A**). Similarly when the scrolls of the Jewish **Torah** are taken out of the **Ark** in the synagogue to be read aloud, men try to kiss them as they pass by.

Even when they are read the Holy Scriptures are often treated in a special way to underline their importance and holiness. Each Jewish scroll, for example, is copied out carefully by hand. When it is being read publicly in the synagogue a metal finger is used so that the reader does not lose his way in the Hebrew text (**B**). Respect is also shown by the place that the Scriptures are given in both private and public worship. In each Christian service at least one, and usually two, readings take place from the Bible, whilst Jews read the entire Torah through in public once a year.

For every religious believer the most important aspect of their Scriptures is the teaching that they contain. Just as God has spoken in the past through the Scriptures so believers expect to hear the voice of God today. This means that they must have absolute authority over the believer's everyday life. The Sikh faith provides a good example of this. Before taking an important decision, a family reads the Guru Granth Sahib through non-stop to allow God to speak to them.

B Why is this man reading from the Torah with a metal finger?

Words to remember

The **Ark** is a cupboard in a synagogue in which the scrolls of the Torah are kept.

The **Guru Granth Sahib** is the Sikh holy book first compiled by Guru Arjan.

The **Qur'an** is the holy book for all Muslims.

The **Torah** is the first five books of the Jewish Scriptures, books of instructions and teaching.

Do you know...

▶ why religious believers often refer to their Scriptures as 'The Word of God'?

▶ how worshippers show respect for the Guru Granth Sahib and the scrolls of the Torah?

▶ why the teaching of the Holy Scriptures is the most important aspect of the holy books?

A key question

How do many religious believers show that they treat their holy books with respect?

Things to do

1 Using the words below, write out and complete the following sentences to show how important the holy books are to religious worshippers.

a They often call their Scriptures the _____ of _____.

b In a gurdwara the _____ _____ _____ is always carried above the heads of the worshippers.

c As the scrolls of the _____ are carried past, Jewish men try to _____ them.

d Religious people try to obey the _____ of their holy books.

Torah   Word   Guru Granth Sahib   teaching
kiss   God.

2 Hidden in this word square are four words or phrases which are found on the opposite page. Find the words and explain, in a sentence, what each of them means (the words can read across or down).

```
F T E R A M J S W N E I H T P
E P D R U X A L Q I P H K A J
L N E W T E S T A M E N T C A
M O Z U N N K U E L N D J R C
N Q L L P D X Z C F G I L O R
G U R U G R A N T H S A H I B
W L A K I J E A O E M N S S I
B L C I Y J I R R N N O R L L
L A R Z N Q U R A N S T K M L
Z H P X O P D V H U Z P Q E N
C H Y F R T O M J H C X Z X E
F W W O T F G S U V B A R O M
```

3 Look carefully at **A** and **B**. They show religious worshippers from two religions showing respect for their own Holy Scriptures. Describe in your own words what is happening in each case.

4 Describe in about a hundred words the different ways in which people try to show that their Holy Scriptures are important to them.

The holy books

2.2 The Jewish Scriptures

A Why do you think that the Torah Scrolls are still copied out by hand?

B Give three examples of books which make up the Torah, the Writings and the Prophets.

To Jewish people their Bible is extremely important. The word 'Bible' itself comes from the Greek word meaning 'books' and that is exactly what the Jewish Bible is. It is a collection of books in the Hebrew language written by many different authors over a long period of time.

Originally the Bible was written on parchment in scrolls and that is still how the Books of the Law (the Torah) are preserved today. You can see this from picture **A.**

The Jews divided their Scriptures into three distinct groups:

▶ The Books of The Teaching (the Torah). The first five books of the Jewish Holy Scriptures (Genesis, Exodus, Leviticus, Deuteronomy and Numbers) form the Torah. This collection of books is the most treasured possession of the Jewish faith. It tells the story of the ancient Israelite nation, how they spent four hundred years in Egyptian slavery, were then delivered from captivity by God through Moses and how, forty years later, they entered the Promised Land of Canaan.

During this journey, called the **Exodus,** Israel received its teaching from God on Mount Sinai and it is this teaching which is recorded in the Torah. Jews today still try to follow this teaching in their daily lives.

▶ The Prophets. The prophets were men and women who spoke to the people on God's behalf. Not all of the prophets had their words recorded in books, but many did. Amongst the most important were Isaiah, Jeremiah and Ezekiel. Although the prophets sometimes spoke of future events they were much more concerned that the people should live God-fearing lives in the present.

▶ The Writings. The third and final division of the Jewish Bible, the Writings, are mainly a collection of poetry and proverbs written by such people as David and Solomon.

When not in use the Torah scrolls are kept in the Ark in the synagogue. The scrolls are normally dressed and capped by a silver crown. During the synagogue service the scrolls are brought out of the Ark and carried in a procession to the lectern (*bimah*). The scrolls are then 'undressed' and the relevant portion read. After the reading, the scrolls are redressed and carried back to the Ark. At the end of their useful life scrolls are not destroyed but are buried in a grave.

Words to remember

The **Exodus** is the name given to the journey of the Israelites out of Egyptian slavery and also to the second book of the Jewish Scriptures which records that journey.

A key question

Which books go to make up the Jewish Scriptures?

Do you know...

▶ which three parts the Jewish Scriptures can be divided into?
▶ where the Torah scrolls are kept in a synagogue?
▶ how Jewish people show their respect for the Torah?

Things to do

1 In Unit 2.1 there is a picture of a Jewish man reading from the Torah. As you can see, he is using a silver pointer to prevent him touching the scroll with his fingers. Can you think of one practical and one religious reason why no one is allowed to touch the scroll with their fingers?

2 In 132 CE the Roman Emperor, Hadrian, forbade all Jews to study or teach the Torah. Rabbi Akiva refused to comply. He said:

> A fox once called the fishes in a stream to come ashore and escape from the big fish that preyed on them. They told him that water is their life-element; if they left it they would surely die. If they stayed some might die but the rest would live.

Akiva went on to explain what he meant:

> The Torah is our element of life. Some of us may perish in the trials of these days but as long as there is the Torah the people will live.

In Akiva's parable:
a Who is the fox?
b Who are the fishes in the stream?
c What is the water?

3 Copy out the following crossword and then fill in the answers. See how many you can do without looking at the opposite page.

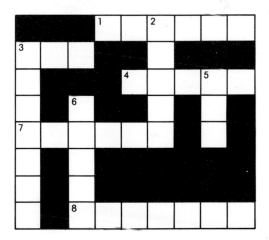

Across
1 The language in which the Jewish Scriptures were written (6).
3 He gave Israel its teaching on Mount Sinai (3).
4 The first five books of the Jewish Scriptures are called this (5).
7 The journey of the Israelites out of slavery (6).
8 Stored in the Ark in the synagogue (7).

Down
2 The word 'Bible' means this in Greek (5).
3 The first book of the Jewish Bible (7).
5 The scrolls of the Torah are kept in this (3).
6 He led the Israelites out of Egypt (5).

The holy books

2.3 The Qur'an

The holy book for all Muslims is the Qur'an. The Arabic word itself means 'recitation', referring to the fact that the contents of the Qur'an were told to the Prophet Muhammad by the Angel Jibrā'il (Gabriel). Originally, of course, the revelations came from God.

There are, Muslims believe, two perfect copies of the Qur'an. The first is in heaven and the other is the one which the followers of the Prophet put together after his death. The Qur'an was written in three stages:

▶ in the course of many revelations the Angel Jibrā'il disclosed to Muhammad the will and mind of **Allah.**
▶ for many years afterwards, Muhammad was followed around by a growing band of companions. They made a note of the revelations by writing them down on scraps of stone, pieces of palm branches and other odds and ends.
▶ a few years after Muhammad's death his friends decided to bring all this material together into a permanent record. The third Khalif (spiritual leader) had four copies of the Qur'an made and these were sent to cities in which there were many Muslim converts.

The words of the Qur'an have never been changed since they were revealed and never will be. The revelation which the book contains remains unaltered. This is why each copy of the Qur'an is carefully transcribed (copied out) and then illustrated by hand. **A** shows a page from an old copy of the Qur'an from the middle of the fourteenth century. The language of the Qur'an is Arabic and this sounds particularly beautiful when it is read aloud. Although the Qur'an has now been translated into many different languages worshippers still try to learn its contents by heart in the original Arabic. They start at about the age of four in special schools arranged by a mosque. The text itself is read from right to left with the reader starting at the top right-hand corner.

In total the Qur'an has over 6000 verses and is about the same length as the Christian New Testament. These verses are divided up into chapters or **Suras** and each chapter has its own title. You can get an idea of the flavour of the Qur'an by reading the verses in the blue box.

The Muslim treats the Qur'an with the greatest possible respect. Before reading it he washes himself carefully. He then unwraps the holy book

A A page from an old copy of the Qur'an. What language is it written in?

B A young Muslim boy learning the Qur'an. Why do you think that he has to start learning the Qur'an so early?

from its cover, reads the passage and then replaces the book carefully on a shelf. It is very important that the Qur'an should always be kept higher than any other book.

Quotations from the Qur'an

The Qur'an provides the Muslim with a guide to daily living. Here are just four quotations from it. Put them into your own words and try to explain what you think they mean.

Children of Allah, wear your best clothes at every time of worship.

You who believe, whenever you intend to pray, wash your faces and your hands up to the elbows, and wipe your head and wash your feet up to the ankles.

You who believe, liquor and gambling, idols and raffles are only a work of Satan, avoid them that you may prosper.

God has permitted trading and forbidden taking interest.

A key question

How did the Qur'an come into being and how do Muslims treat it today?

Words to remember

Allah is the Muslim name for God (who reigns alone and has no rivals).

A **Sura** is one of the 114 chapters in the Qur'an.

Do you know...

▶ what the word 'Qur'an' means?
▶ how many perfect copies of the Qur'an there are?
▶ how the Qur'an came to be written?

Things to do

1 Copy this downword into your book and fill it in by answering the clues.

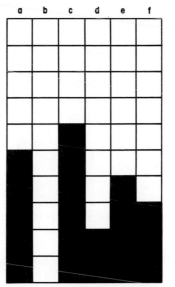

a The sacred book for all Muslims (5).
b The word Qur'an means _____ (10).
c A chapter of the Qur'an is called a _____ (4).
d The Qur'an is a collection of revelations given by God to _____ (8).
e The original language in which the Qur'an was written (6).
f The angel who revealed the Qur'an to Muhammad (7).

2 Here is a verse from the Qur'an. Copy it into your book and then explain why Muslims are not allowed to query the Qur'an.

This Qur'an could not have been composed by any but Allah . . . It is beyond doubt from the Lord of Creation. If they say 'It is your own invention' say 'Compose one chapter like it'.

3 According to Muslim tradition the followers of Muhammad recorded the Qur'an from:

. . . scraps of parchment and leather, tablets of stone, ribs of palm branches, camels' shoulder blades and ribs, pieces of board and the breasts of men.

Most of the things in this quotation are things you could write on but how do you think the followers got teachings from the 'breasts of men'?

2.4 The Hindu holy books

A In this illustration from the Mahābhārata Krishna is seen as the chariot-driver of Arjuna. Who were Krishna and Arjuna?

B What are Krishna and Arjuna talking about in this illustration from the Bhagavad Gita?

C Who is Rama killing in this illustration from the Ramayana and why?

There are many Hindu holy books. They are divided into two groups. These are:

▶ The **Shrutis** ('what is heard'). The Shrutis are the **Vedas** which are the oldest books known to man. The Vedas are those compositions which Hindus believe to have come directly from God himself. Revealed originally to the holy men of India, the Vedas have been passed down from teacher to pupil for centuries. The **RigVeda** (one of the four Vedas) contains 1028 hymns to various Hindu gods.

▶ The **Smritis** ('what is remembered'). These are the holy writings which Hindus have remembered and passed on from generation to generation. As the human memory is far from perfect so these writings are not considered to be as important as the Shrutis.

The **Purana** and **Itihasa,** part of the Smritis, tell of Hindu legend and history. Amongst them is the **Mahābhārata** — the oldest and longest poem in any language. You can see an illustration from one version of this poem in **A.** It has three million words and tells the story of two sets of royal cousins who quarrel over who should succeed to the throne. Finally they go to war. Arjuna, one of the cousins, hates war but is an excellent warrior. In the final battle he hesitates because he does not want to kill members of his own family. He orders his chariot driver to withdraw from the battle. Arjuna is very surprised when his driver begins to argue with him. Then he realises that his driver is none other than **Krishna,** a god, who has come to live on earth. Krishna tells Arjuna that those who die in battle are not dead for ever. The prince believes him and leads his forces to victory. **B** shows Krishna in conversation with Arjuna.

C is an illustration from a version of the **Ramayana** which is one of the two great Hindu epic poems. It tells the story of Rama, a god, who visits the earth and marries Princess Sita. She is then abducted by Ravana, a fierce demon, and taken to the island of Lanka. After fierce fighting Rama rescues her and they are restored to their thrones.

The theme of both the Mahābhārata and the Ramayana is also the basis for most stories in the Hindu Scriptures. It is that good will always triumph over evil even though evil often appears to be winning the day.

The Laws of Manu

The Laws of Manu is an old Hindu book. It was written between 200 and 100 BCE. In its twelve sections there are many laws which cover the everyday behaviour of the Hindu. Here is a short extract:

Coveting the property of others, thinking in one's heart of what is undesirable, and adherence to false doctrines [beliefs] are three kinds of sinful mental action. Abusing others, speaking untruth, detracting from the merits of all men and talking idly shall be four kinds of evil verbal action.

a Try to put this quotation from the Laws of Manu into everyday English. You might need a dictionary to help you at times.

b Give examples from your own experience of:
   i 'speaking untruth'
   ii 'detracting from the merits of all men'
   iii 'talking idly'.

c Using the examples given in the quotation to help you, can you think of another type of 'sinful mental action' and another type of 'evil verbal action'?

A key question

What is a very important theme that runs through most of the Hindu Scriptures?

Do you know...

▶ which is the most important group of Hindu Scriptures?
▶ which is the longest Hindu poem and what it is about?
▶ what the Ramayana is about?

Words to remember

Krishna is one of the most popular of the Hindu gods.

The **Mahābhārata** is the longest Hindu epic poem, containing almost 100,000 verses.

The **Purana** and **Itihasa** are those Hindu holy books which record legend and history.

The **Ramayana** is one of the oldest epic poems in the Hindu religion, with 24,000 verses.

The most sacred of the Hindu Scriptures is the **RigVeda** which contains more than 1000 hymns in praise of the many Hindu gods.

The **Shrutis,** one division of Hindu holy books, are those in which God is believed to have spoken directly with men.

The **Smritis,** another division of Hindu holy books, are those which have been written down and recorded from memory.

The **Vedas** are the earliest collection of Hindu holy books, collected some time between 1500 BCE and 800 BCE.

Things to do

1 Match up the words in the left-hand column with their correct meaning from the right-hand column.
   a Vedas   i   'what is heard'
   b Shrutis   ii   Hindu god
   c Smritis   iii Hindu prince
   d Mahābhārata   iv   'what is remembered'
   e Krishna   v   oldest poem in any language
   f Arjuna   vi   oldest books known to man

2 The Bhagavad Gita, a greatly-loved part of the Hindu Scriptures, forms part of the Mahābhārata. **B** is taken from a version of the Gita. Using the information that you are given in this unit describe in your own words what the picture shows.

3 Draw a picture which shows your own idea of good triumphing over evil.

The holy books

2.5 The Living Guru

It was Guru Arjan who compiled the Adi Granth in 1604. The original composition is now to be found in the Gurdwara Shish Mahal at Kartarpur District, Jullundur in India. Guru Arjan collected together the teachings of his four predecessors and combined them with contributions from various Muslim and Hindu holy men to form the Adi Granth, so illustrating the Sikh belief that truth is not to be found exclusively in one religion. Sikhs today remain convinced that there are many paths to God.

Shortly before he died, in 1708, the tenth and last of the Gurus, Guru Gobind Singh, added the writings of his father, Guru Tegh Bahadur, to the Adi Granth to form the holy book of the Sikhs — the **Guru Granth Sahib.** He also told the people that there were going to be no more gurus (spiritual teachers) to lead them. From now on their only guru would be the Guru Granth Sahib. Since then the presence of this holy book has been necessary for all acts of worship and Sikh weddings. For any building to be recognised as a gurdwara it must contain a copy of the Guru Granth Sahib.

The Guru Granth Sahib is at the centre of every act of Sikh worship and is given the greatest possible respect by all those taking part. When young babies are brought into the gurdwara a random reading of the Granth is the basis for choosing their names. Marriages are performed in front of it. On moving to a new house or into new business premises, the Guru Granth Sahib is installed there for an hour or so and a few passages from the Granth are read before asking for God's blessing.

For a long time Sikhs resisted all attempts to have copies of their holy book printed. This was because

A This shows the Guru Granth Sahib being read in a gurdwara. Are there any signs in this picture of the great respect shown by Sikhs towards their holy book?

B A passage from the Sikh creed. What is this creed called and in which language is it written?

they did not want the Granth to be sold through bookshops and so handled by non-Sikhs in a casual way. Today any Sikh who is going to come into contact with the Granth must take a bath and wash their hands before turning its holy pages. When a copy of the Guru Granth Sahib is printed it must be the exact length of the original. Each page must contain the same number of words and the book as a whole must have 1430 pages.

The most important passage in the Guru Granth Sahib comes at the beginning. It is the Sikh creed (the **Mool Mantra**) and can be translated as:

> There is but one God. Truth by name, the creator, all-pervading spirit, without fear, without enmity. Whose existence is unaffected by time, who does not take birth, self-existent, who is to be realised through his grace.

You can see from **B** just how this creed looks in the Guru Granth Sahib. It is written in Punjabi, the language in which the Sikh Scriptures are printed.

A key question

Why do Sikhs give such a high degree of importance to their holy book, the Guru Granth Sahib?

Words to remember

The **Guru Granth Sahib** is the holy book for all Sikhs, containing the compositions of the Sikh Gurus and the writings of non-Sikh holy men of India.

The **Mool Mantra** is the Sikh statement of belief taken from the Guru Granth Sahib.

Do you know...

▶ who compiled the Adi Granth?
▶ what the relationship is between the Adi Granth and Guru Granth Sahib?
▶ how the Guru Granth Sahib is treated by Sikhs?

Things to do

1 Here is a word puzzle. Copy it into your book and fill it in by answering the clues given below.

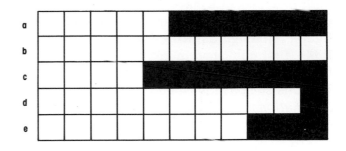

a The guru who compiled the Adi Granth in 1604 (5).
b The guru who added the teachings of his father to the Adi Granth in 1708 (6, 5).
c The word for a spiritual teacher (4).
d What the Sikh creed from the Guru Granth Sahib is called (4, 6).
e A Sikh place of worship (8).

2 Sikhs believe that wherever the Guru Granth Sahib is found you have a gurdwara. **A** shows this holy book being read in a gurdwara. Describe, in your own words, three ways in which Sikhs have shown, and continue to show, great respect towards their holy book.

3 Someone has commented that Sikhs honour the Guru Granth Sahib without actually worshipping it. What do you think they meant?

4 Look carefully at the translation of the Mool Mantra on the opposite page. It contains ten statements about God. Make a list of them. What do you think that the creed means by each of the following statements about God?
a 'all-pervading spirit'
b 'whose existence is unaffected by time'
c 'who does not take birth'
d 'self-existent'
e 'who is to be realised through his grace'.

You might need your teacher's help with one or two of these phrases.

Unit 3 The Bible

3.1 What is the Bible?

By any standards the history of the **Bible** is very impressive. Since 1800 no less than three thousand million copies of it have been printed and, each year, a further ten million copies are added to this figure. Although the **King James Version** of the Bible, first published in 1611 (**A**), is still popular it has been overtaken in recent years by more modern versions such as the *Good News Bible,* the *New International Version* and the *Revised English Bible.*

But what of the Bible itself? The Bible is divided into two parts:

▶ the Old Testament. For centuries the books of the holy Jewish Scriptures have formed the Christian Old Testament. Here we find, in all, 39 different books which were written over a time-span of at least a thousand years. We do not know the names of many of the authors or editors. Exploring this collection is one way of beginning to understand the Christian religion since these books form the background to so much of what is written in the New Testament.

▶ the New Testament. This part of the Bible is mainly concerned with Jesus of Nazareth – the Messiah – whose coming was prophesied in the Old Testament. In the New Testament there are two main kinds of writing; history and letters.

The historical writing includes the four **Gospels** (Matthew, Mark, Luke and John), which describe the life, teaching and death of Jesus. Luke, the doctor, who travelled throughout the Roman Empire with Paul, not only wrote one of the Gospels but also a description of the Early Church which is called the Acts of the Apostles.

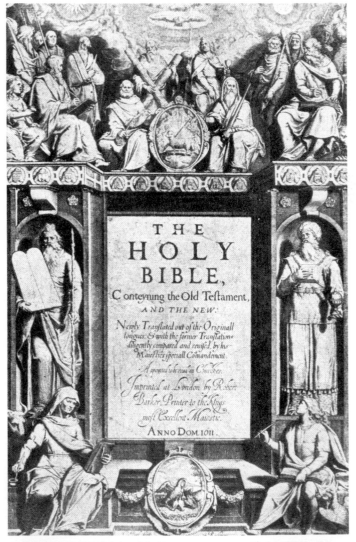

A The title page from a 1611 edition of the King James Bible. Can you find out why the Bible was translated at this time?

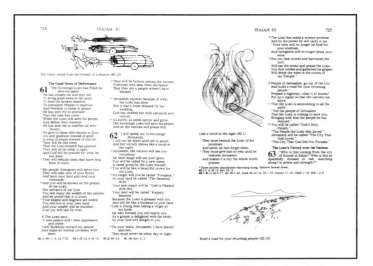

B Pages from the modern *Good News Bible.* Why should people want the Bible translated into modern English?

The letters (or **Epistles**) were written to guide and help the early followers of Jesus. Most of them were written by Paul, although letters are also included from, amongst others, Peter and John.

What binds all these writers and their very different books in the Bible together? The answer is that many Christians believe the Bible to be 'God-breathed'. This means that the writers themselves were 'inspired' as they wrote and so the books that they have left behind carry for Christians an authority which no other writings have.

Words to remember

The word **Bible** comes from the Greek word meaning 'books' and is used by both Christians and Jews to refer to their Holy Scriptures.

An **Epistle** is a letter contained in the New Testament which was written by one of the apostles of Jesus.

The word **Gospel** means 'good news' and refers to those four books in the New Testament which describe the life and teaching of Jesus of Nazareth.

The **King James Authorised Version** of the Bible was completed by a team of scholars in 1611 and placed in every church in the country by King James I.

Do you know...

▶ which translation of the Bible was published in 1611 and who authorised it?
▶ which part of the Bible Christians share with Jews?
▶ which two kinds of writings go to make up the New Testament?

A key question

What makes the Bible carry more authority for Christians than any other book?

Things to do

1 The Bible makes some important claims for itself. Here are just three of them:

We know that what the scripture says is true for ever . . .

John 10.35 (*Good News Bible*)

¹²For the word of God is living and active. Sharper than any double-edged sword, it penetrates even to dividing soul and spirit, joints and marrow; it judges the thoughts and attitudes of the heart.

Hebrews 4.12

. . . from infancy you have known the holy Scriptures, which are able to make you wise for salvation through faith in Christ Jesus. ¹⁶All Scripture is God-breathed and is useful for teaching, rebuking, correcting and training in righteousness, ¹⁷so that the man of God may be thoroughly equipped for every good work.

2 Timothy 3.15,16

As the Bible was not completed until well after these verses were written, they can only refer to the Old Testament. They do, however, sum up how some Christians feel about the whole Bible.
a Which word is used three times in these verses to refer to the Old Testament?
b Which phrase is used here to refer to the Old Testament?
What does it suggest to you about the Old Testament?

2 The Bible is widely used in this country in national, political, social and personal life. Can you think of FIVE ways in which the Bible is used regularly?

3 The Bible appears in the *Guinness Book of Records* as the most widely published book of all time. Yet someone has said:

'The Bible is the most widely published and the least read book in the world.'

Do you think that they are right?

4 a What kind of material would you find in the four gospels?
b Who wrote most of the epistles, and why were they written?

The Bible

3.2 How was the Bible put together?

Many of the accounts in the Bible began as stories. These were kept alive for centuries as parents passed them on to their children. Obviously, as they were passed down, some details were altered but all the evidence suggests that the Hebrews, like other ancient people, had excellent memories. As time went on, however, so the tradition of recording important pieces of information and keeping them carefully developed. When, for example, Moses received the Ten Commandments on Mount Sinai they are said to have been written on 'tablets of stone' which were then stored in a sacred box (the Ark) in the **Tabernacle** (**A**). The ancient Jews took the Tabernacle with them wherever they went.

Later on, the words of many of the prophets were written down by their disciples and then kept alive either by word of mouth or by being recorded. Jeremiah, one of the most important prophets, had his own secretary, Baruch, who recorded everything that he said. At about the same time **Psalms** were written to be used in worship in the **Temple**. **B** shows an artist's impression of what this building, built originally by King Solomon, might have looked like.

By the time of Jesus all of the books of the Old Testament had been collected together to form the

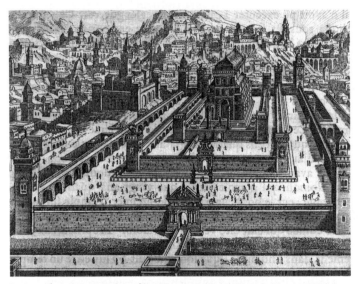

B An artist's impression of the Temple built by King Solomon. Which other king rebuilt the Temple in Jerusalem?

A Why was this portable shrine, the Tabernacle, carried by the Jews throughout their forty years in the wilderness?

C Modern Jewish scrolls. Which scrolls from the Jewish Scriptures are most important to Jews today?

Jewish Scriptures. There was still some debate, however, as to whether or not some of them should be included, but the matter was settled at the Synod of Jamnia, held in 90 CE.

When the first Christians met together after Jesus had left the earth they continued to use the Jewish Scriptures as most of them were Jews by birth. At the same time they talked amongst themselves about Jesus and his teaching. They thought it was particularly important to listen to those people who had heard Jesus teaching, especially his disciples. Before long, however, these people began to die. There was a real fear that their memories would die with them. **Mark,** followed by Luke and **Matthew,** each wrote down a record of the life and teaching of Jesus as they understood it. They did so on scrolls similar to those that you can see in **C.**

These were not, however, the earliest written Christian documents. Already Paul had written many letters to churches and individual Christians. Because of Paul's authority these were read and treasured by the early believers.

Gradually a collection of books emerged. These were added to the Old Testament to form what we know as the Bible. At two councils, held in the fourth century, the Church's seal was finally put on those books which now form the Bible.

Words to remember

Mark was a follower of Jesus and the author of the first Gospel to be written.

Matthew, a tax collector, was a disciple of Jesus and the author of a Gospel.

Psalms were Jewish songs sung in praise of God.

The **Tabernacle** was a portable shrine in which the ancient Israelites kept the sacred objects of their religion as they travelled across the desert to the Promised Land.

The **Temple** was a very large building in Jerusalem first erected by King Solomon and then rebuilt, much later, by King Herod.

A key question

How was the Bible put together?

Do you know...

► how the ancient Jews kept, and stored, important pieces of information?
► the names of the followers of Jesus who wrote the Gospels in the New Testament?
► who wrote the earliest Christian documents in the New Testament?

Things to do

1 Copy and complete the sentences below:
  a The Ten Commandments were said to have been given to Moses on _____ of _____.
  b The _____ was a kind of portable shrine which the Jews took with them wherever they went.
  c When eye-witnesses began to die _____, _____ and _____ wrote down their accounts of the life and teaching of Jesus.
  d _____ wrote many letters and these are some of the earliest Christian documents.
  e It was not until the _____ century that the composition of the Bible was finally decided.

2 Look at drawing **B.**
  a Trace the drawing into your book.
  b Underneath write TWO sentences about the Temple using the information that you are given in this unit.

3 The Gospel accounts of the life of Jesus are drawn from information provided by eye-witnesses, especially the disciples. Imagine yourself to have been one of these eye-witnesses and describe the impact that the three years you spent with Jesus before he left the earth has had. Here are some Bible references that might help you:

► Matthew 8.23–27
► John 11.1–44
► John 13.12–17

3.3 The Bible into English

A The beginning of Mark's Gospel in the Lindisfarne Gospels. Who produced this translation?

C John Wycliffe, leader of the Lollards, with some of his followers. What part did Wycliffe play in translating the Bible into English?

B The ruins of the Lindisfarne Priory on Holy Island, off the Northumberland coast.

The whole of the Bible was not translated into English until the end of the fourteenth century. Well before then, though, parts of it had been translated into local dialects. Very frequently an English translation was written underneath the Latin text. A beautiful example of this is the **Lindisfarne Gospels** (**A**). These were produced by the monks who lived at Lindisfarne on Holy Island (**B**).

In the fourteenth century, John Wycliffe and his followers began to call for a translation of the Bible into English. They argued that only the local priest could read Latin and that as the Bible belonged to the people it should be available in their everyday language. His followers, the **Lollards,** set about translating the Bible and copying it out by hand. About two hundred copies of their work are still in existence.

When the first book was printed in 1454 the demand to print the Bible increased. The people had to wait until 1526 for this to happen and, even then, it was only the New Testament that was printed. This was the work of **William Tyndale** who had to print the book in Germany and smuggle it into England hidden in bales of wool and wine casks. Tyndale had said that:

> 'A boy who drives the plough in England shall know more of the Bible than many priests.'

Although Tyndale himself was burnt at the stake in Belgium in 1536 it was not to be long before the whole Bible was available in English.

Miles Coverdale, in 1535, produced the first English printed Bible. Within three years a copy of the Bible was placed in every parish church in the country. The Bibles were so valuable that they were chained to a desk to prevent thieves from taking them.

The most famous translation of all was printed in 1611. It was sponsored by King James I and became known as the King James Authorised Version. For the next three hundred years it was to stand almost unchallenged as 'The Bible'. It is still used today on official occasions and in many churches.

Words to remember

The **Lindisfarne Gospels** were a very early illustrated translation of the four Gospels in the New Testament.

The **Lollards** were followers of John Wycliffe who wanted to translate the whole Bible into English.

William Tyndale was responsible for the first translation and printing of the New Testament in English.

Miles Coverdale was responsible for the first printing of the whole Bible in English.

Do you know...

▶ what the Lindisfarne Gospels were?
▶ how John Wycliffe and his followers contributed to the translation of the Bible into English?
▶ what parts were played by William Tyndale and Miles Coverdale in the printing of the Bible?

A key question

Why was it considered so important to have the Bible translated, and printed, in English?

Things to do

1 **A** shows the beginning of Mark's Gospel in the Lindisfarne Gospels. As you can see, the text was illuminated (decorated) with very great care. This has also been true of other versions of the Bible.

   a Copy out a verse from the Bible and decorate it in the style of the Lindisfarne Gospels.

   b William Tyndale, amongst others, was prepared to die in his fight to have the Bible translated into English. Why do you think that he saw his task as being so important?

   c Why do you think that such great care has always been taken of the Bible?

2 At the end of the Lindisfarne Gospels the monks involved in the translation added this footnote:

   > Eadfrith, Bishop of the Church at Lindisfarne, he at the first wrote this book for God and St Cuthbert and for all the saints in common that are in the island, and Ethilwald, Bishop of those of Lindisfarne Island, bound and covered it outwardly as best he could. At Bilfrith the anchorite he wrought as a smith the ornaments that are on the outside, and adorned it with gold and with gems, also with silver overgilded, a treasure without deceit. And Alfred, an unworthy and most miserable priest, with God's help and Cuthbert's, overglossed it in English . . .

   a What impression do you get from this quotation of the teamwork which was needed to produce the Lindisfarne Gospels?

   b Can you find any clue in the quotation as to who might have written these words?

3 Imagine that you and a friend are involved in the early work of translating the Bible into English. Both the King and the Church are opposed to what you are doing. Describe some of the dangers of your work and the steps that you might take to ensure that the Bible is printed and that copies of it can reach those who want to read it.

3.4 Many translations of the one book

By 1611, when the King James Authorised Version of the Bible was published, there had already been many different translations of the Bible. Then, for some 250 years, the work of translating largely stopped. It was only revived towards the end of the nineteenth century when some very old manuscripts of the Old and New Testaments came to light. These were much older, and more valuable, than those on which the King James Version had been based. Generally speaking, the older a manuscript is the more reliable it is thought to be.

In 1844 and 1859 Count Tischendorf made two visits to the monastery of St Catherine on Mount Sinai (**A**). Here he was astonished to discover many priceless manuscripts. Amongst them were the oldest Biblical manuscripts yet known. These have been called **Codex Sinaiticus.** In 1933 these were bought by the British Government and are now in the British Museum. In 1885 a new translation of the Bible, the **Revised Version** was published. However, it was still very much like the old Authorised Version. It was not until 1903 that Richard Weymouth published the first New Testament 'in everyday English'.

As the Second World War ended in 1945 there was a great interest in the Bible but J.B. Phillips, an Anglican clergyman, found that young people in his parish could not understand the Bible in any version then available. He set out to paraphrase the New Testament in words that were familiar to them. This translation became extremely popular throughout the country and it is still used today.

Nothing, however, could rival the success of the **Good News Bible.** Originally written in America for people who used English as a second language, eight million copies were sold in its first year of publication. This put it at the top of the bestseller lists for many months. Today over eighty million copies of the *Good News Bible* have been printed. Apart from its easy-to-read text the attraction of the *Good News Bible* has been its unusual illustrations (**B**).

A St Catherine's monastery on Mount Sinai. What was found here, by whom and when?

B An illustration from the *Good News Bible*. When was this version of the Bible published?

Back in 1961 the New Testament of the **New English Bible** was published, to be followed five years later by the Old Testament. This translation became particularly popular for reading aloud in public Christian worship. In the years that followed a committee of scholars worked on yet another revision and this was finally published in 1989. This **Revised English Bible** is the newest translation to be offered to readers of the Bible.

Words to remember

Codex Sinaiticus is a very old Biblical manuscript. Codex is the name for an early form of book made by sewing leaves of writing material together.

Known at first as 'Today's English Version', the **Good News Bible** was published in two parts with the New Testament in 1966 and the whole Bible in 1976.

A committee of eminent scholars produced the **New English Bible** in its complete form in 1966.

The **Revised English Bible,** published in 1989, is a new, up-to-date revision of the *New English Bible*.

When the **Revised Version** of the Bible was published in 1885 the same language as the Authorised Version was kept but some alterations were made in the light of new manuscripts.

A key question

Why have there been many modern translations of the Bible?

Do you know...

▶ why many new translations of the Bible have appeared since the Authorised Version?
▶ how Codex Sinaiticus came to light?
▶ which popular translations have been published since the Second World War?

Things to do

1 The drawing in **B** accompanies the story of the temptation of Jesus in Matthew 4.3. Read this story for yourself and then:
   a Retell the story in your own words OR
   b Produce a drawing of your own to illustrate the story in a style similar to that in the *Good News Bible.*

2 These different translations of the same verses from the New Testament (Hebrews 1.1,2) show how the text of the Bible has changed over the years.

   ▶ **Tyndale (1526):** God in tyme past diversly and many wayes, spake vnto the fathers by Prophets: but in these last dayes he hath spoken vnto vs by his sonne, whom he hath made heyre of all things, by whom also he made the worlde.
   ▶ **Authorised Version (1611):** God who at sundry times and in divers manners spoke in time past unto the fathers by the prophets, hath in these last days spoken to us by his Son, who he hath appointed heir of all things, by whom also he made the world.
   ▶ **J.B. Phillips (1947):** God, who gave to our fore-fathers many different glimpses of the truth in the words of the prophets, has now, at the end of the present age, given us Truth in the Son. Through the Son God made the whole universe and to the Son He has ordained that all creation shall ultimately belong.
   ▶ **The *Good News Bible* (1976):** In the past, God spoke to our ancestors many times and in many ways through the prophets, but in these last days he has spoken to us through His Son. He is the one through whom God created the universe, the one whom God has chosen to possess all things at the end.

   a Do you think that updating the language of the Bible is helpful or not? Give reasons for your answer.
   b Do you think that one version is more suitable to be read in church than any others?
   c Is it important that the Bible should be in the everyday language of the people?

The Bible

3.5 The Bible worldwide

In December 1802 a Welsh minister, Thomas Charles, was very concerned that the Bible had not been translated into his native tongue. Arising out of this concern the British and Foreign Bible Society was formed two years later. Its stated aim was:

> 'To encourage the wider circulation of the Holy Scriptures, without note or comment.'

By 1817 similar Bible societies had been formed in Scotland, Ireland, Canada, Russia, Denmark, Holland, Sweden, Norway and Australia. By the end of the century over two hundred million Bibles, New Testaments and smaller parts of the Bible were in circulation throughout the world. There was also a great effort to translate the Bible into as many different languages as possible.

During the twentieth century this work of translation has largely been carried out by the **Wycliffe Bible Translators.** Formed in 1934, this movement is now the largest Missionary Society in the world, with over three thousand missionaries scattered across every continent. Since their formation the Wycliffe Bible Translators have published the whole, or part of, the Bible in over seven hundred different languages and dialects. There is much work still to be done, however, before the Bible can be read by everyone. In Mexico alone there are 137 local dialects whilst Papua New Guinea boasts 152!

By looking at **A** and **B** you can get some idea of how the work of translating and distributing the Bible has changed in recent years. In **A** an early Bible distributor is carrying copies in two trunks at the end of a pole. In **B** a Nigerian and a missionary are working together on a translation

A Why do you think that many of the early Bible distributors, like this one in Malagasy, were willing to risk their lives to distribute the Bible?

B A European missionary is working with a Nigerian to translate part of the Bible. How successful have the translators been in translating the Bible so that everyone in the world can read it in their own tongue?

of a part of the Bible into a local dialect. These days most of the translation work is done, if possible, by local people so that the text can be as close as possible to their own spoken language.

Since the invention of printing parts of the Bible have been translated into almost 2000 different languages and dialects. Yet that still leaves millions of people in the world who do not yet have the whole Bible in their native tongue. Clearly the work of translating the Christian Scriptures will need to go on for a long time to come.

C Why do you think that it is important for these Kenyan students to be able to read the New Testament in their own language?

Words to remember

The **Wycliffe Bible Translators,** formed in 1934, translate and distribute the Bible throughout the world.

A key question

How much of the world today has the Bible, or part of it, translated and printed in their own language?

Do you know...

▶ how the British and Foreign Bible Society was formed and for what reason?
▶ what work is carried out today by the Wycliffe Bible Translators?
▶ how translators go about their work of translating the Bible into as many different languages as possible?

Things to do

1 Imagine that you are living in the country shown in **A** fifty years ago. You have been asked to accompany the Bible distributor shown in the picture on one of his journeys.
   a What kind of preparations do you think might be necessary before you set out?
   b What problems might you encounter?
   c What kind of reaction do you think you might get from the villagers that you meet?

2 Imagine that you are the missionary in **B.** You have been sent to Nigeria to help translate one of the Gospels into a local dialect.
   a What would be the first thing that you would do?
   b What do you think would be the main problems of translating a Gospel into an unknown foreign tongue?
   c How would you set about your task?
   d How do you think a native of the country could help you?

3 In **C** two young Kenyan women are reading the New Testament in their own tongue. Imagine that these two women have just become Christian believers. What difference do you think it might make to them to have the Bible in their own tongue?

4 In the quotation on the opposite page we learn that the British and Foreign Bible Society was set up in 1802:

   'to encourage the wider circulation of the Holy Scriptures, without note or comment'.

   Why do you think that the distribution of the Bible was to be 'without note or comment'?

3.6 What is the Bible all about?

The first chapters of the Book of **Genesis** (the book of 'beginnings') pose and seek to answer some very important questions:

▶ how was the universe created?
▶ where did the first people come from?
▶ what is humanity's relationship with God?
▶ what is a man's relationship with his wife?
▶ what is humanity's relationship with animals and the rest of creation?
▶ why is there sin (wrong-doing) in the world?

According to the book of Genesis the first man and woman were created by God in a state of innocence. Sin entered the world when the woman gave in to the serpent's temptation and persuaded her husband to do so as well. They were banished from their perfect garden.

This **myth** begins the story that runs through the rest of the Bible. It is the story of a people, the Jews, who were chosen by God. Abraham, the father of the Jewish nation, made an agreement with God that his descendants should worship God alone. Abraham's grandson, Jacob, was renamed 'Israel' and his twelve sons became the fathers of the twelve tribes of Israel.

A According to this sixteenth century woodcut, and the book of Genesis, the first man and woman lived in an idyllic garden. What do you think is the truth behind this myth?

B A sixteenth century illustration of St Michael defeating the dragon. On whose side is St Michael and what does the dragon represent?

Through the many centuries that followed the Jews spent a long time in slavery. God sent many people (among them Moses, Ezra and Nehemiah) to lead them out of slavery at different times in their history. Each time, despite their good intentions, God's people failed to live up to the teaching that God had given to them.

Then came Jesus. His followers believed that he was God's son, the Messiah, or the chosen leader of the Jews. As an adult he was baptised by John the Baptist in the River Jordan. For a short time Jesus taught his disciples and the people about God before being put to death by the Roman authorities. However, the New Testament insists that after three days Jesus was brought back to life. This is the most important event in Christian history.

After Jesus left the earth his followers formed themselves into the Christian Church. The details of what happened then takes up the second part of the New Testament. Christians believe that the story which began so long ago is still going on today as the followers of Jesus continue to spread his message.

Words to remember

Genesis is the first book of the Bible and records the story of the creation and the early characters in the story of Israel.

A **myth** is a traditional story. In the Bible myths teach important lessons about God and man.

A key question

What is the central theme running through the Bible?

Do you know...

▶ which questions are posed by the early chapters of the Bible?

▶ what story runs through the Bible?

▶ what part Jesus plays in the main drama of the Bible?

Things to do

1 Copy out and complete these sentences:
   a _____ is the book of beginnings.
   b The Bible is the story of a people, the _____, who were chosen by God.
   c It was _____ who made an agreement with God that his descendants would worship God.
   d _____'s twelve sons became the fathers of the twelve _____ of Israel.
   e God sent many people to rescue the Jews from slavery including _____, _____ and _____.
   f His followers believed that Jesus was God's _____, the _____.

2 Look carefully at **A**. It contains many symbols. The woodcut illustrates the story in the third chapter of Genesis. You will need to consult that story before you are able to answer some of these questions:
   a What do you think that the unicorn in the picture symbolises?
   b What are the man and the woman both holding in their left hands? Who has picked it first? Is it important?
   c How can you tell that the scene illustrated took place before the man and the woman sinned?
   d What is the symbol of evil in the woodcut? Why do you think that it was given a human face?

3 **B** shows a scene from the last book in the Bible, the Book of Revelation, in which St Michael, the Archangel, is fighting the dragon. This continues the theme which is introduced at the beginning of the Bible — the conflict between good and evil.
   a Why do you think that evil is symbolised by a dragon in this picture?
   b Where is the battle between the powers of good and evil taking place?
   c What do you think the artist is trying to convey by the scene that has been shown underneath the conflict?
   d Describe one incident in the life of Jesus which is concerned with this conflict. Here are some examples to help you:
      ▶ Matthew 4.1–11
      ▶ Mark 11.15–18
      ▶ Mark 14.43–46.

Unit 4 Religious worship

4.1 Worshipping on the Sabbath Day

A A service is taking place in a Jewish synagogue on the Sabbath day. Write down three things that you notice about this service.

The Jewish **Sabbath,** or Shabbat, begins at sunset on Friday evening and runs through until the stars appear in the sky on Saturday evening. During this time the Jew is forbidden to do any work. Instead he or she delights in the rest that God has provided. As this quotation from the Talmud (a book of ideas based on the Torah) shows, the Sabbath is looked upon as one of God's greatest gifts to the Jewish people:

> God said to Moses, 'I have a precious gift in my treasure house. "Sabbath" is its name. Go and tell the people of Israel that I wish to give it to them.'

So, in the morning on the Sabbath, Jews make their way to the nearest synagogue. Most of them will walk rather than use their car or public transport. The service in the synagogue can only begin when a **minyan** [ten men] are present. In most synagogues men and women sit separately and the children sit either with their mother or their father.

Each person follows the service in their **Siddur** [prayer book]. One of the most important parts of the service takes place when the Ark is opened, a scroll is taken out and carried to the **bimah.** It is a great honour to be called up to read from the Torah then and to say the blessing over the reading. The cover, crown and breastplate are then replaced on the scroll before it is taken back to the Ark.

During the service psalms (religious songs) are sung by the congregation from the Jewish Bible. No musical instruments can be played on Shabbat because that would be considered work for the musicians. Instead, each place of worship has its own song-leader, called a **cantor** (or **hazan**). Prayers also form an important part of each act of Jewish worship and many are said during the Shabbat service, including the **Shema** and the **Amidah.** The Shema is taken from Deuteronomy 6.4–9 and is the basic statement made by all Jews of their belief in God. You can find the Shema in the blue box.

Words to remember

The **Amidah** is a series of eighteen benedictions (or prayers of blessing) which form the core of Jewish worship.

The **bimah** is a desk or platform in a synagogue from which the Torah is read.

The **cantor** or **hazan** is the song-leader in the synagogue.

Minyan is the Hebrew word meaning 'count' indicating the minimum number of men which make a service congregational.

The **Sabbath** is the seventh day, a day of rest for all Jews. It is the day which symbolises God resting after six days of creating the world.

Siddur is the title of the daily Jewish prayer book.

The word **Shema** means 'hear' and refers to the first word of Deuteronomy 6.4.

The Shema Deuteronomy 6.4

Hear, O Israel: The Lord our God, the Lord is one.
You shall love the Lord your God with all your heart and with all your soul and with all your might

▶ What does the Shema say about God and what does it say about man's response to God?

A key question

How do Jews celebrate their Sabbath day?

Do you know...

▶ what a minyan is?
▶ what the Sabbath day is?
▶ what the Shema and the Amidah are?

Things to do

1 Copy into your book and learn the Shema off by heart. Then answer these questions:
  a To which nation is the Shema addressed?
  b What do you think the words 'the Lord our God, the Lord is one' mean?
  c Why do you think that the people are told to love God 'with all your heart and with all your soul and with all your might?'
  d Explain why the Shema is very important to all Jews.

2 Here are some words taken from this unit. Explain in just one sentence what they mean:
  a A minyan
  b A Siddur
  c The bimah
  d The cantor or hazan
  e The Shema.

3 The Amidah prayer contains 18 blessings. It is said every day as well as the Sabbath. Here is just a short extract:

   O Lord, open my lips and my mouth shall declare your praise. Blessed are you, O Lord our God and God of our Fathers, God of Abraham, God of Isaac and God of Jacob, the great, mighty and revered God, the most high God who bestows loving-kindnesses and possesses all things; who remembers the pious deeds of the patriarchs and in love will bring a redeemer to their children's children for your name's sake.

  a Which three people from the Jewish Scriptures are described as the 'Fathers' of the Jewish people?
  b Make a list of all the things that this extract says about God.

4 A rabbi (religious teacher) who lived in the tenth century had this to say about the Sabbath:

   'The Sabbath is an opportunity to achieve rest from the abundance of one's toil so that one may acquire a little knowledge and pray a little more, and so that people might meet together and discuss matters of Torah . . .'

According to this rabbi the Sabbath rest allows a Jew to do five things. What are they?

4.2 Worshipping in the mosque

In Muslim countries the **Mu'adhdhan** climbs to the top of the **minaret** five times a day to issue the call to prayer. In this country the Call still goes out but is usually made from inside the building. Wherever it is said, the words are always the same — you can find them in the colour box.

All male Muslims must attend the mosque for prayers at midday on Fridays unless they are ill or are travelling in a country where there are no mosques. On entering the mosque they must remove their shoes as a sign of respect for Allah. Although most men wash at home before going to the mosque, facilities are provided for people to go through the washing ritual — washing hands, rinsing mouth and nostrils, washing arms to the elbow, lightly wiping the forehead, ears and neck before washing the feet to the ankle. This procedure is repeated three times and is very important. It means that the worshipper is both physically and spiritually clean before entering the presence of Allah.

Washing over, the worshipper can enter the mosque to pray to Allah. The Prophet Muhammad described prayer as:

> '. . . a stream into which the faithful worshipper dives five times day.'

A What direction are the prayer mats facing, and what is included in the design?

B What is a Rak'ah and how does it express a man's condition in God's presence?

Just as water cleanses the outside of a person's body, so prayer cleanses his soul. The prayers in the mosque are led each Friday by the **Imam** and he takes all of the worshippers through the **Rak'ah.** During the Rak'ah each worshipper faces downwards (once) and prostrates himself on the ground (twice). At those moments he is showing respect and total submission to the will of Allah.

It is always preferable for a Muslim man to pray in a mosque — especially during the Friday prayer. Yet it is not essential. He can pray to Allah anywhere. When he is praying elsewhere he will use a **prayer mat** since that guarantees that he is praying in a clean place. Often the mat is of a plain colour and has a pattern with an arch in it which can be pointed in the direction of Makka (Mecca).

Muslim women must pray in the same way as men but they do not have to do so in a mosque. Many have domestic responsibilities and it is most important that they should not neglect them. They are encouraged, therefore, to say their prayers at home so that they can continue to look after the rest of the family.

Words to remember

The **Imam** is the leader of public prayer in the mosque.

The **minaret** is the tower attached to a mosque from which the Mu'adhdhan calls the faithful to prayer.

The **Mu'adhdhan** is a person who summons the faithful to prayer five times each day.

By laying out his **prayer mat** the Muslim guarantees that the ground on which he is praying is clean.

The **Rak'ah** is the Muslim ritual of repeating set prayers together with appropriate movements.

A key question

What is the central element in all Muslim worship and how does the Muslim carry it out?

The Call to Prayer

God is the greatest. God is the greatest. God is the greatest. God is the greatest.
I bear witness that there is no God but Allah.
I bear witness that there is no God but Allah.
I bear witness that Muhammad is the messenger of Allah. I bear witness that Muhammad is the messenger of Allah.
Come to prayer. Come to prayer.
Come to security. Come to security.
God is the greatest. God is the greatest.
There is no God but Allah.

▶ What is the Muslim name for God?
▶ Who was God's messenger?
▶ Where is the Muslim to go for prayers?
▶ Why do you think that each phrase is repeated at least twice?

Do you know...

▶ how often the Call to Prayer is issued and what is said?
▶ why washing is a very important part of prayer?
▶ how male responsibilities in prayer differ from those for females?

Things to do

1 Find an illustration of a prayer mat.
   a Either copy this drawing into your book or, better still, design your own prayer mat.
   b Underneath your drawing explain why a Muslim needs to use a prayer mat.

2 The main emphasis in Muslim worship is upon the greatness and mercy of God and the weakness and needs of man.
   a How is this brought out in the Muslim approach to prayer?
   b Compare the call to prayer with the Christian Lord's Prayer.
      i Are the two prayers similar?
      ii Do they approach God in a similar way?
      iii What are the main differences?

4.3 Sikhs worshipping

On entering a gurdwara Sikhs remove their shoes and sit cross-legged on the carpeted floor for worship. Each man must wear his **turban** and each woman a **dupatta**. Having bowed low in front of the Holy Book they then present their gift of food or money, together with a silk cloth to cover the Holy Book, if they wish to.

Anyone, male or female, can conduct a Sikh act of worship since there are no priests. Everyone is considered to be equal in the sight of God and so equally capable of leading an act of public worship. The service itself can last for any length of time between one and five hours. During this time the worshippers are free to come and go as they please although everyone is expected to be present as the service draws to a close.

Unless someone is reading from the Guru Granth Sahib it is kept covered during the service. The **granthi** sits behind the Holy Book throughout the service and waves a special fan or **chauri** over it. This underlines the authority that the Guru Granth Sahib is believed to have.

Men and women worship together, although they sit separately in the hall. Hymn singing is a very important part of a Sikh service and this is often accompanied by musicians using a harmonium and a pair of small drums. At the end of the service everyone stands and faces the Guru Granth Sahib to listen to the Common Prayer. This is called the **Ardas** and you can find a short extract in the colour box.

Finally the **karah parshad** is given to the congregation. This is cooked in the gurdwara kitchen and brought into the hall before the close of the service. It is touched with a kirpan (sword) before distribution (**A**). The fact that everyone then eats together demonstrates that all people are equal and united in their faith. Karah parshad also shows that no one is allowed to leave the Guru's presence empty-handed.

After the service everyone gathers for a communal meal in the **langar.** People sit in rows to eat, with the men and women still separate. The object of the meal is to bring together all members of the Sikh community and to break down any barriers that there might be between them.

A Karah parshad being distributed in a gurdwara. Why do Sikh services always end in this way?

The Ardas Prayer

O True King, O Loved Father, we have sung Thy sweet hymns, heard Thy life-giving Word . . . may these things find a loving place in our hearts and serve to draw our souls towards Thee. Save us, O Father, from lust, wrath, greed, undue attachment and pride . . . Give us light, give us understanding, so that we may know what pleases Thee, Forgive our sins . . .

▶ Which two names are applied to God in this prayer?
▶ Which five things does the worshipper ask God to save him from?
▶ What three things does the worshipper ask God to do for him?

B These Sikhs are playing musical instruments as part of their worship. Looking at them, how would you know that they were Sikhs?

Words to remember

The **Ardas** is the prayer which forms a part of every Sikh service.

The **chauri** is a yak-hair or peacock-feather fan waved over the Guru Granth Sahib during a service in the gurdwara.

A **dupatta** is a scarf worn as a head-covering by Sikh women in a gurdwara.

The **granthi** is an official in a gurdwara whose work it is to read the Guru Granth Sahib and perform religious ceremonies.

Karah parshad, the food shared by the congregation after a gurdwara service, is a mixture of flour, sugar and ghee (clarified butter).

The **langar** is a kitchen attached to the gurdwara and also refers to the free meal served there.

A **turban** is a head-covering worn by Sikhs which has religious significance.

A key question

What aspects of Sikh faith are stressed during a service and the meal that follows it?

Do you know...

▶ which symbols of the Sikh faith men and women wear to the gurdwara?
▶ what the main features of a service in a gurdwara are?
▶ what happens at the end of a service and what it represents?

Things to do

1 People often share a meal with friends to celebrate a special occasion like a birthday or a wedding.
   a Write down FIVE other occasions on which people might eat a meal to celebrate something special.
   b Why do you think that friends celebrate a special occasion by eating together?
   c What religions do you know of which include a meal in their service?

2 Sikh people do not set aside a special day for worship, although in this country most gurdwaras hold their services on a Sunday. Why do you think that some religions stress the importance of having one special day each week for worship and others do not?

3 Here is one Sikh describing his weekly visit to the gurdwara:

   'Everyone starts by saying the hymns from our Holy Book and ends by joining in a special meal. As we worship God together our children are allowed to wander around freely just as they like. To be truthful there is a lot of movement throughout the service as people come and go all the time. We are used to this but visitors find that it is rather strange. The end of the service is the most important time and all of the worshippers are expected to be there for that.'

   a Which kind of religious service would you most like to attend — one that was strictly organised or one that was far more casual?
   b Why?

4.4 Hindus worshipping

The attitude of Hindus towards public worship is rather different from that of the other religions. Worship begins at home for every Hindu. Each morning when they get up they have a good bath. They cannot pray until their bodies are clean.

Then many Hindus pay a visit to their local temple (**A**). They can go there on their own or as a family. Men, women and children all worship together. Once at the temple there is no set form of religious worship as you will find in a church on a Sunday or in a synagogue on the Sabbath day. Instead Hindus simply gather with other worshippers in front of the shrine to perform a **puja.** This can vary from shrine to shrine but it usually involves a worshipper presenting the god or goddess with a gift of sweets or flowers. The priest then presents each worshipper with a blessed offering, **prasad,** and makes a mark on the worshipper's forehead (**B**) with red powder.

A short time of silence then follows when each worshipper can offer up their own silent prayers before the sweets that have been placed before the statue are returned. The worshipper eats a small part of them before distributing the remainder to everyone present in the temple — rich and poor.

Acts of worship like these can be performed at any time. At the moment there are few Hindu

A Inside a Hindu temple. What is distinctive about this place of worship?

temples in this country, although some Hindu groups are now either building their own temples or converting existing buildings. As Hindus are free to worship God anywhere such worship can take place in a temple or at the shrine in the home. The temples, however, are important religious as well as social centres for many Hindus.

B This Hindu is wearing the mark of the god Shiva on his forehead. Why do you think that the mark is placed there?

Words to remember

Prasad is a blessed offering in Hinduism.

Puja is a common form of worship.

A key question

What is distinctive, and unusual, about a Hindu act of worship?

Do you know...

► where worship begins for every Hindu?
► what a puja is?
► what a Hindu offers to the god or goddess when he or she visits a temple?

Things to do

1 Write out and complete the following sentences using the information in this unit:
   a _____ and _____ are often presented as offerings to the Hindu gods.
   b The priest presents each worshipper with a _____ _____ which is also called a _____.
   c One of the marks which a priest might make upon the worshipper's forehead is the _____ of _____.
   d Before attending an act of worship in a temple each Hindu will _____ thoroughly.
   e A puja is performed in front of the _____.

2 Many Hindus in this country do not attend a temple regularly. Here is one young Hindu girl who lives over here with her family describing a visit which she had recently made back to India:

   'When I was in India a few weeks ago my parents took me to see many Hindu temples but I wasn't too sure what to make of them. My Mum told me that if we still lived in India then we would visit the temple every day to say our prayers. That is the custom over there.

   In this country, however, things are very different. We do not have a temple anywhere near to where we live and so we just pray to God wherever we might be — in the house or in the open-air.'

   a Do you think that a young Hindu might find it difficult to practise his or her religion without going anywhere near a temple?
   b What do you think would be the advantages for a Hindu in meeting other Hindus in a temple if that were possible?

3 Write down the similarities and differences of worship in the four religions that you have read about in this unit. Here are some guidelines to help you:

   ► when do they worship?
   ► where do they worship?
   ► what happens in their services?
   ► do they have a religious leader and what does he/she do?
   ► is there a meal as part of the service and what is it like?

Unit 5 Christian worship

5.1 Christians worshipping

Religious worship is the practical way in which people can express how they feel about God. As Christian belief centres around Jesus Christ, so his name frequently occurs in Christian worship. This is most clearly seen in the service of **Holy Communion,** which is the most important service in most Christian churches. You can find out more about this in Unit 5.3.

A Christian act of worship does not have to take place in a church. In recent years more and more Christians have worshipped together in 'house churches'. Most Christians, however, still prefer to join in their acts of public worship in a church building. The singing of hymns, the reading of the Bible, praying and listening to a **sermon** are all part of this worship. Through these things the Christian believer is not only seeking forgiveness for past sins but is also looking to God for help to live a better life in the future.

The need to worship is felt by all Christians yet the form that worship takes varies considerably from church to church. All of the churches have their own pattern of Christian worship:

▶ The older Christian churches tend to follow a set pattern taken from their own particular prayer book. For example, in the Church of England congregations followed, until recently, the services in the **Book of Common Prayer.** This was written in 1662. Most congregations now, however, use the **Alternative Service Book.** Roman Catholics and Orthodox Christians have their own prayer books.

▶ The Free Churches, such as the Methodists and Baptists, do not have a prayer book but prefer the **minister** to lead their worship as he or she chooses. **A** shows a minister leading a Sunday service in a Methodist church.

▶ Some smaller churches do not have a minister or recognised leader to direct the worship. These groups, such as Plymouth Brethren and the Quakers, depend upon someone in the congregation being 'led by the Spirit' to lead the worship. Often in a Quaker meeting most of the time is taken up with private, silent prayer.

A This service is taking place in a Methodist Church. What are two important differences between this service and one that might be taking place in an Anglican Church?

B What is the distinctive feature of worship for Quakers?

Words to remember

The **Alternative Service Book,** now used in most Anglican churches, was drawn up in 1980.

The **Book of Common Prayer** was drawn up in 1662 to lay down the services that could be held by the Church of England.

Holy Communion is the title applied by the Church of England to the service which recalls the death and resurrection of Jesus.

Free or Nonconformist churches usually call their leader a **minister.**

A **sermon** is the talk given by the priest or minister in which some aspect of Christian belief and behaviour is explained.

A key question

Do all Christians worship in the same way or are there considerable differences between them?

Do you know...

► what the most important service of worship is in most churches?
► what the *Book of Common Prayer* is?
► what elements go to make up most acts of Christian worship?

Things to do

1 Look at photographs **A** and **B**. Describe carefully what you think is going on in each picture.

2 Give the right word for each of these definitions:
   a A group of people who have come together to worship God in a church (a c_____).
   b The practical way in which people express what they believe about God (w_____).
   c The most important Christian service (H_____ C_____).
   d The part of the service in which a minister might explain a passage from the Bible to his congregation (a s_____).

3 In this unit several reasons are given for Christians coming together to worship. What are they?

4 In this extract a young Christian is describing why the service of Holy Communion is so important to her:

   'In our church when we celebrate Holy Communion we are all remembering that the Lord Jesus Christ died, was buried and rose again from the dead three days later. To me the most important part is the belief that he rose again. This means that one day he will return to this earth again. Every time we celebrate Holy Communion we are being reminded of this fact.'

   a Which three events does this young Christian remember every time that she celebrates Holy Communion?
   b What does she consider to be the most important part of Holy Communion?
   c What does she say that every Christian is looking forward to when he or she celebrates Holy Communion?

Christian worship

5.2 Places of worship

There are some Christians who do not think that the place in which they worship is of any significance at all. They are just as happy meeting in a community centre or a home as they are in a church. Others try to keep their place of worship as simple as possible — such as the Plymouth Brethren and the Quakers.

The majority of Christians, however, do attach a higher degree of importance to their place of worship. They regard it as sacred or holy with a character and an atmosphere which must be preserved. It is this which allows worshippers to sense the presence of God and to respond to it with a mixture of reverence and awe.

Although Christian places of worship vary greatly in age and character most of them do have certain characteristics in common:

▶ Many places of worship are beautiful. This is particularly true of those buildings which are called **cathedrals.** It is believed that the beauty and furnishings of such buildings help people to worship God.
▶ The focal point in Anglican, Roman Catholic and Orthodox churches is the **altar.** This is the place from which the services are conducted and the Eucharist is dispensed. When people face the altar they are facing east where the sun rises, symbolising the resurrection of Jesus from the dead.
▶ In most church services there is a preacher who delivers his or her sermon from the **pulpit.** This sermon plays a most important part in Nonconformist services and the pulpit acts as the focus of such churches. The pulpit is above the level of the congregation so that the preacher can be heard and seen by everyone in church.
▶ Inside many older churches there are often symbolic elements designed to point the worshipper towards God. For example, the shape of the church may be in the form of a cross; there may be stained-glass windows which were designed to tell stories from the Bible and stories of the saints at a time when most people could not read; a **font** which holds the water which is used to baptise babies may stand inside the door of the church. Its position emphasises that baptism is the door to the church family.

In addition to these general features most denominations have their own distinctive features as well. Baptist churches have a baptistry (for adult baptism) at the front of a church. Roman Catholics have a **confessional** in their churches so that a priest can hear the confessions of members of his congregation.

A What acts as the focal point in this Methodist chapel? Can you find out why?

A key question

What are the main features to be found in most Christian places of worship?

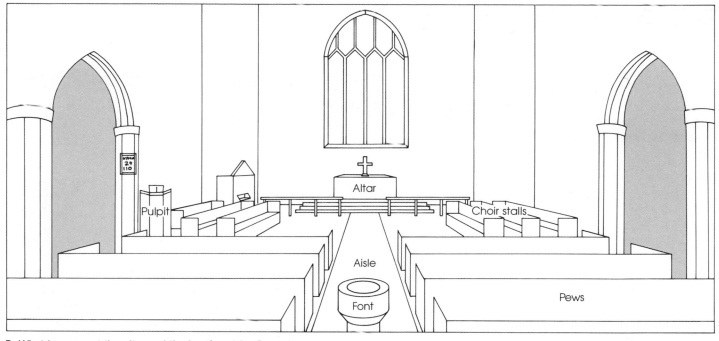

B What happens at the altar and the baptismal font?

Words to remember

In most older churches the **altar,** the 'holy table', is at the end of the nave.

The word **cathedral** comes from the Latin word meaning 'the throne of the bishop'. It is the church over which a bishop presides.

The **confessional** is a wooden cubicle which separates a person who is confessing their sins [the penitent] from the priest who is listening.

Usually found just inside the door of a church, the **font** is the stone receptacle used to hold the water for baptism.

The **pulpit** is the raised platform in a church from which the sermon is given.

Do you know...

▶ what is distinctive about a cathedral?
▶ which feature is the focal point of most Anglican churches, and which feature draws the attention of worshippers in a Nonconformist church?
▶ which distinctive features are to be found in Baptist and Roman Catholic churches?

Things to do

1   In this unit several technical words have been used to refer to features in Christian places of worship. Explain what each of the following means in not more than two sentences:
   a   The altar
   b   The font
   c   The pulpit
   d   Stained-glass windows.

   If possible, arrange a visit to your local church. Draw two of these objects and try to find out as much as you can about their history. Is there any interesting feature in the church that we have not mentioned? If so, discover as much as you can about it.

2   Places of worship are usually full of symbolism. Copy **B** into your books and explain why it was thought appropriate to build older churches in the shape of a cross. Then find out the answers to these questions:
   a   Why do churches have spires and what do they symbolise?
   b   What is the location of the altar in most older churches and what does this symbolise?
   c   What are the main differences between the churches shown in **A** and **B**?

5.3 The Eucharist or the Mass

A Worshipper receive the wafer of bread during the Roman Catholic Mass. What do they believe happens to this wafer and the wine that they drink?

The most important service in most Christian churches is the special meal in which Christians share together their belief that after Jesus was crucified he came back to life. According to the Gospels this took place on the first day of the week, the Sunday, after the Jewish Sabbath or Shabbat. Most Christians meet together regularly to share bread and wine just as Jesus taught his disciples to do in the last meal that he ate with them before he was crucified. You can read an account of this in the blue box.

Although the different Churches celebrate this same event they do so in their own way and call it by different names:

▶ Roman Catholics call the service **Mass** and they believe that during the most sacred part of the service the bread and wine are actually turned into the broken body and blood of Christ. So, each time the Mass is celebrated, the sacrifice of Jesus is re-enacted [**A**].

▶ Anglicans prefer to call their celebration the **Eucharist** or Holy Communion. Although some Anglicans hold beliefs similar to those of Roman Catholics [they are called 'High' Anglicans] and others are much closer to the Nonconformists [called 'Low' Anglicans], most eat a wafer of bread and take a sip of wine as a memorial of that last supper which Jesus ate with his disciples.

▶ Many Nonconformists call their celebration the **Lord's Supper** or **the breaking of bread.** To them the bread and the wine are symbols which help them to remember the death of Jesus and what it means to them personally.

So the service is known to Christians by many names. To many of them it is also a **sacrament,** an outward sign by which God's presence and blessing can be channelled to them. Not everyone, though, sees the Eucharist in this light. There are some Christian groups, most notably the Salvation Army and Quakers, who do not celebrate it at all.

1 Corinthians 11.23–26

²³For I received from the Lord what I also passed on to you: The Lord Jesus, on the night he was betrayed, took bread, ²⁴and when he had given thanks, he broke it and said, "This is my body, which is for you; do this in remembrance of me." ²⁵In the same way, after supper he took the cup, saying, "This cup is the new covenant in my blood; do this, whenever you drink it, in remembrance of me."

▶ What did Jesus tell his disciples after he had broken the bread and what do you think he meant by what he said?

▶ What did Jesus say to his disciples as he gave them the wine and what did he mean by it?

Words to remember

Some Nonconformists use the term **breaking bread** because, at the Last Supper, Jesus 'broke bread' with his disciples.

The term **Eucharist** is one of several used by Christians to describe their central act of worship and means 'thanksgiving'.

It was Paul who first called the service of remembrance the **Lord's Supper** and this title is still used by many Nonconformists.

The word **Mass** comes from the last words of the old Latin service – 'Ite missa est' – meaning 'Go, it is finished'.

A **sacrament** is an outward, visible sign of an inward, spiritual blessing obtained through a service of the Christian Church such as Holy Communion or baptism.

A key question

Why is the Eucharist or Mass the most important act of Christian worship?

Do you know...

▶ what a sacrament is?
▶ which event in the life of Jesus is recalled in the Eucharist?
▶ why Christians break bread and drink wine during the Eucharist?
▶ what the main differences are between the ways that Roman Catholics, Anglicans and Nonconformists approach the Eucharist?

Things to do

1 Here are several words used in this unit. Explain each of them in not more than two sentences.
   a The Mass
   b The Eucharist
   c A sacrament
   d Holy Communion
   e The Lord's Supper
   f The Sabbath

2 The *Alternative Service Book* of the Church of England was published a few years ago and is now used in most Anglican churches. It offers these two forms of the same prayer:
   a Accept our praises, heavenly Father, through your Son our Saviour Jesus Christ, and as we follow his example and obey his command grant that by the power of your Holy Spirit these gifts of bread and wine may be to us his body and blood.
   b Hear us, O most merciful Father,
   we most humbly beseech thee;
   and grant that by the power of thy Holy Spirit
   we receiving these thy creatures of bread and wine,
   according to thy Son our Saviour Jesus Christ's holy institution,
   in remembrance of his death and passion,
   may be partakers of his most blessed body and blood.

   Which of these two prayers is much older than the other? How can you tell? What are the main differences between them? Which do you prefer? Why?

5.4 Leaders in the Church

Not all Christian Churches have professional, full-time leaders who receive a salary for their work. There are those, like the Quakers, who draw their leaders from amongst the congregation. Whilst this allows each member of the congregation to use their special gifts in the service of others and God, it is very much the exception. Although most churches do make use of members of the congregation there are certain services – most notably the Eucharist – which can only be carried out by a priest. In the case of the Methodist Church the Eucharist service must be performed by a fully ordained minister.

Each Church retains its own way of training and **ordaining** its priests. The training itself is often long. To train for the Roman Catholic priesthood, for instance, takes six years. At the end of the training the priest takes a vow of **celibacy.** No other Church requires celibacy from its priests, arguing that as most of the congregation will be married it is reasonable that the priest should be married as well.

The Roman Catholic, Anglican and Orthodox Churches have what is called an **episcopal** form of ministry. This means that they are ministered to by **bishops.** Above the bishops in the Roman Catholic Church is the **Pope**, whilst the leader of the Anglican Church is the **Archbishop of Canterbury.** Below bishops are priests who carry out their work in parishes. Sometimes **deacons** are also attached to parish churches and are able to conduct most services — but not the Eucharist.

There are no woman priests in the Roman Catholic and Orthodox Churches, nor are they likely to ordain women in the foreseeable future. Some Churches – such as the Episcopal Church in the USA, the Methodist and the Baptist Churches – already ordain women to the priesthood. A tremendous tussle has taken place in the Church of England as to whether women should be ordained. Although the issue has caused deep division in the Church it appears likely that there will be ordained women priests in the Anglican Church by the end of the twentieth century.

A This church leader is entering a church to conduct a confirmation service. Why do you think that he is carrying a shepherd's crook?

B What do you think are the main tasks which a priest or minister should carry out in today's world?

A key question

Who are the main leaders in the Christian Church?

Words to remember

The first **Archbishop of Canterbury** was Augustine. For centuries the holder of this position has lived at Lambeth Palace.

Celibacy is the rule that priests should abstain from sexual relationships.

A **deacon** can perform most services in the Church of England, but not the Eucharist.

When a Church has an **episcopal** form of ministry it means that the senior positions in the Church are held by **bishops.**

Ordination is the ceremony by means of which each Church accepts a person as a priest or minister. A bishop will lay his hands on the person to transfer to them the power and authority of the Church.

The **Pope** is the Bishop of Rome and the chief bishop in the Roman Catholic Church.

Do you know...

▶ what ordination is and why many Christians consider it to be very important?
▶ who is the head of the Roman Catholic Church and who is the head of the Anglican Church?
▶ which Churches accept women priests and which do not?

Things to do

1 Answer each of these questions in your own words using the information that you have been given in this unit.
   a Can you name one Church that does not have ministers or priests?
   b Why can a Bishop alone ordain people to the priesthood?
   c What does it mean when a Roman Catholic priest takes the vow of celibacy?
   d What is a deacon?
   e What is the name of the area over which a priest exercises jurisdiction?
   f What does it mean to say that a church has an episcopal form of ministry?

2 The *Book of Common Prayer* includes these words which are spoken by the bishop to the priest who is being ordained:

   A priest is called by God to work with the bishop and with his fellow-priests, as servant and shepherd among the people to whom he is sent. He is to proclaim the word of the Lord, to call his hearers to repentance, and in Christ's name to absolve and to declare the forgiveness of sins. He is to baptise . . . He is to preside at the celebration of Holy Communion . . . He is to lead his people in prayer and worship . . . He is to minister to the sick and prepare the dying for death . . .

   a Which two words are used here to describe the way that the priest should work amongst the people and what do you think they mean?
   b A whole list of tasks for the priest are set out here. What are they?

Unit 6 Prophets, saints and gurus

6.1 The Jewish prophets

In early Jewish history a **prophet** was a man or a woman who was believed to have been inspired by God. Sometimes these prophets would foretell future events but, more usually, they told the people what God was saying about their wrong-doing. Probably the first of these prophets was **Moses.** His sister, Miriam, was a prophetess and so was another woman from early Jewish history called Deborah (**A**).

Later on, the prophets were to play a very important part in Jewish history. There was Amos, a herdsman by profession, who suddenly appeared in the market-place and started preaching the judgement of God to the people. Another prophet, Hosea, used his own life to illustrate how loving and forgiving God is. His wife had been unfaithful to him and he told the Israelites that they, too, were being unfaithful to God by worshipping other gods. But just as he took his wife back, so God will always welcome people who are sorry they turned away from him.

Then followed a whole succession of prophets who told the nation of Israel in no uncertain terms that God would judge them. Isaiah declared that God was holy and the nation of Israel was full of hypocrites who carried out all the religious laws and rules scrupulously but neglected the poor and helpless. In fact this theme was taken up by several of the prophets. When Jeremiah preached a critical message, however, he was branded a traitor and thrown into prison.

Nor was he the last of God's messengers to suffer. Perhaps the most well-known is Daniel, who was thrown into a lion's den because he refused to stop praying at the king's command. Like Jeremiah, though, Daniel survived because God was with him. So, too, did Jonah who ended up being

A What kind of things might this woman, a prophetess, be telling the people?

B Can you piece together some of the story of Jonah from this wall carving?

swallowed by a great fish because he refused to preach God's word to the people of Nineveh.

Although most of the prophets lived almost 3000 years ago they are not forgotten by Jews today. Apart from the Torah (the Books of Teaching), no part of the Jewish Bible is more highly valued by Jews than the Prophets. This is divided into two sections:

▶ **The Major Prophets:**
Isaiah
Jeremiah
Ezekiel

▶ **The Minor Prophets:**

Daniel	Nahum
Hosea	Habakkuk
Joel	Zephaniah
Amos	Haggai
Obadiah	Zechariah
Jonah	Malachi
Micah	

Passages from the Prophets are read after Torah readings during synagogue services.

Words to remember

Moses was the great leader and law-giver during the time that the Jews left their slavery in Egypt and travelled to the Promised Land.

A **prophet** was a person who spoke to the people of Israel the word of God.

A key question

What was the basic message that the prophets declared to the people of Israel?

Do you know...

▶ what a prophet is?
▶ who was believed to have been the first Jewish prophet?
▶ how Jews keep the message of the prophets alive today?

Things to do

1 Unscramble the words in brackets and then copy out the complete sentences:
   a Men who spoke on behalf of God to the Jewish people were called (THPOSERP).
   b The first Jewish prophet was probably (ESMOS).
   c The prophet who likened Israel to his own faithless wife was (SOEHA).
   d (BREADHO) was a prophetess.
   e (RJIAEMEH) was a prophet who ended up in prison.

2 Here is an answered crossword. Copy it out. Under your copy write down clues for each of the answers:

3 Imagine that a prophet, like one of those that you have read about, were to visit this country today.
   a What kind of things do you think he would have to say?
   b Are there any things that he would be very happy about?
   c Which things do you think he might be particularly unhappy about?

You could illustrate your answer with cuttings from newspapers and magazine articles. You might like to extend this into a wall display of the things which concerned the prophets of old and the things which concern people today.

4 Read Jonah 1.1–2.10 and look at picture **B**. Describe the events in Jonah's life which you can see in the carving.

Prophets, saints and gurus

6.2 The saints

A **saint** is a person in the Christian religion who has shown outstanding love for God and holiness during his or her life. Often, although not always, a saint was also a **martyr** who was put to death for his or her religious beliefs. Whether or not they met a violent death miracles came to be associated with the burial places of most saints.

The first recorded Christian martyr was **Stephen** whose death by stoning is recorded in the Acts of the Apostles. Some years later both St Peter and St Paul died violently. Although little is known about the actual circumstances it seems fairly certain that both of them were put to death during an anti-Christian persecution initiated by the mad Roman Emperor, Nero, in 64 CE.

In the years that followed most of the original disciples of Jesus were martyred. Then, in 155 CE, the Christian leader Polycarp was slaughtered. After his death his bones were collected together by his followers and said to be:

'. . . more precious than jewels of great price . . .'

The bones were buried in a safe place but dug up again when his disciples met to celebrate his death. The death-day [natalis] of a martyr was always considered to be very important because this day was believed to be the person's birth-day in heaven as they were reunited with Christ through their death.

It soon became the custom to bury the bones of a

A This engraving shows Stephen being stoned to death. You can read about this in Acts 7.54-60. Why was he stoned to death?

B This illustration shows the Christian leader Polycarp. What happened after his death?

martyr under the altar in a church. This was thought to be the most appropriate place for a servant of Christ to end his days. At the same time the bones, or **relics,** of the saint were thought to have particular healing properties. Thousands of people travelled from shrine to shrine as pilgrims hoping to be cured of various ailments and illnesses. These relics were also thought to protect the churches that housed them. In the Middle Ages churches often competed against each other to own the relics. Large sums of money frequently changed hands for them.

Since then many of the most popular saints have been largely forgotten. Others, however, still live on in the names of our parish churches.

Words to remember

A **martyr** is a man or a woman who is put to death because of their religious convictions.

A **relic** is a bone of a saint or an object associated with a saint which is believed to have mysterious healing powers.

Stephen was the first Christian saint who was put to death. This happened after he preached a sermon in Jerusalem testifying to his faith in the risen Christ.

A **saint** is a person in the Christian religion who is thought to have lived a particularly holy life and with whom miracles are often associated.

A key question

Why have saints played an important role in Christian history?

Do you know...

▶ what a saint is?
▶ what a martyr is?
▶ what relics were and why they were thought to be so important?

Things to do

1 Copy out these sentences and fill in the blanks from the words below.
   a A _____ is someone who has laid down his or her life for their religious beliefs.
   b After the death of a saint miracles were often associated with their _____.
   c Both St _____ and St _____ are believed to have died at the hands of the mad Roman Emperor _____.
   d The bones of St _____ were said to have been 'more precious than jewels of great price.'
   e The death-day of a martyr was known as the _____.
   f The custom in the Middle Ages was to bury the bones of a saint under the _____ of a church.

   altar   Peter   Polycarp   Paul   martyr
   burial places   Nero   natalis

2 Find out which saint your local church is dedicated to and then discover as much as you can about that saint.

3 Explain in your own words the meaning of:
   a Saint   c Natalis
   b Martyr   d Relics

4 Shortly before he was martyred St Polycarp was given the opportunity of turning his back upon the Christian faith. He is said to have replied:

   'For eighty-six years I have been his (Christ's) servant and he has never done me wrong; how can I blaspheme my king who saved me?'

   What do you think that Polycarp meant when he said this?

5 An ancient writer describes the death of Polycarp in the following way:

   When the crowd at the games in the amphitheatre was told that Polycarp had confessed that he was a Christian they shouted first for the lions and then for him to be burnt at the stake. He was bound; an official killed him with his sword; his body was then burnt.

   Imagine that you are St Polycarp. Write an account of the last few minutes of your life and the thoughts that are going through your mind at the time.

6.3 The Sikh Gurus

In Sikhism the status of a **Guru** (spiritual teacher) is regarded very highly. Guru Nanak (1469–1539) was the first Guru and Guru Gobind Singh [1666–1708] was the last. You can find a complete list of the ten Gurus in the blue box.

Guru Nanak died in 1539. He chose one of his followers, Bhai Lehna, to succeed him. He gave him the name Angad [my limb]. Angad made the Punjabi language known to the common people so that they could understand the many hymns of Guru Nanak.

When Guru Amar Das, who succeeded Angad, became leader he insisted that every Sikh place of worship should have a kitchen attached [**A**]. Here the rich and poor could eat alongside each other. Guru Ram Das founded the holy city of Amritsar, which is the most sacred of all Sikh places of worship. It was left to Guru Ram Das' successor, Guru Arjan, to build the Golden Temple there (**B**) and also to prepare the Holy Book, the Guru Granth Sahib, for all Sikhs to read. Guru Arjan was also the first Sikh to die for his faith. Burning sand was poured over his body by Turkish Muslims before he was made to sit in very hot water and then roasted to death. Guru Hargobind introduced a martial spirit into Sikhism so that the faith could be defended, if necessary.

The seventh and eighth Gurus were able to live peaceful lives but the ninth, Guru Tegh Bahadur, was beheaded by a Muslim Emperor of India for asserting his right to freedom of worship. During the time of the tenth and final Guru, Guru Gobind Singh, the followers of Guru Nanak underwent a severe persecution. In 1699 Guru Gobind Singh called all Sikhs together in Anandpur. With a drawn sword he asked them:

'Is there anyone who will give up his head to prove his faith in me?'

One man volunteered, went into the tent with Guru Gobind Singh, there was a thud and blood poured out under the tent flap. This happened four more times with further volunteers, but then all five men came out from the tent. They had passed their toughest test and were the first members of the Sikh brotherhood of the **Khalsa** [the pure ones].

Words to remember

A **Guru** is a holy man and a spiritual teacher in the Sikh faith.

The **Khalsa** is the Sikh brotherhood, founded by Guru Gobind Singh, to which men and women are admitted after an initiation ceremony.

A Can you find out why a kitchen is a very important part of every Sikh place of worship?

B Who had the Golden Temple at Amritsar built?

C To which brotherhood does this Sikh belong?

The Sikh Gurus

Guru Nanak	died 1539
Guru Angad	died 1552
Guru Amar Das	died 1574
Guru Ram Das	died 1581
Guru Arjan	died 1606
Guru Hargobind	died 1644
Guru Har Rai	died 1661
Guru Har K'ishan	died 1664
Guru Tegh Bahadur	died 1675
Guru Gobind Singh	died 1708

A key question

What special contributions to Sikhism were made by the ten Gurus?

Do you know...

► who was the first Sikh guru?
► who built Amritsar and who began work on the Golden Temple there?
► which Sikh Guru was responsible for founding the Khulsa?

Things to do

1 Study the information in this unit. Copy out these sentences and fill in the blanks:
   a Gurus are _____ men and _____ in the Sikh faith.
   b As neither of his sons was fit to succeed him Guru Nanak chose _____ to whom he gave the name _____ meaning _____ _____.
   c It was _____ _____ who founded the city of Amritsar.
   d Guru Arjan prepared the Holy Book, the _____ _____ _____, for Sikhs to read. He also built the _____ _____ at Amritsar.
   e Guru _____ and Guru _____ were both put to death for their faith.
   f Guru _____ _____ founded the Sikh brother-hood called the _____ which means the _____ _____.

2 Imagine that you were one of the five men who volunteered to enter the tent with Guru Gobind Singh.
   a Describe how you might have felt as you made up your mind and went towards the tent.
   b Imagine that you were a relative of one of these men. Describe your feelings as you heard the thud and saw the blood flowing out of the tent.
   c Describe what you felt as the men came walking out of the tent with Guru Gobind Singh.
   d Why do you think that Guru Gobind Singh carried out this test?
   e What was he trying to find out about the men?

Unit 7 Symbols in religion

7.1 Symbols in religious worship

A The altar-cross in a church. Why do you think that so many people have found the cross to be a powerful symbol?

Symbols are a very important part of religious worship. Without them such worship would be impossible. This is because, in all religions, God is so great that he cannot, in himself, be known. Human language is totally inadequate to describe him. Unless he is to remain unknown, then, symbols must be found which will at least make him partly knowable.

Take, for example, the Christian belief about God. To Christians God is an all-powerful, invisible and loving spirit. As such he is totally beyond all human experience. Some link, therefore, between God and human experience had to be found to bridge this gap. One useful symbol that Christians have found is to call God their 'Father'. They were taught to do this by Jesus. You will remember that he began the prayer that he taught his disciples to pray with the words:

'Our Father, which art in heaven . . .'.

B What symbol is visible in this synagogue?

Yet even that is not as simple as it sounds. What do Christians mean when they refer to God as their 'Father'? Obviously it does not mean that God has fathered them in the same way as their human fathers have done. What Christians really mean is that God acts towards them as a perfect father could be expected to treat his children — firmly with discipline and yet lovingly and tenderly. In this way the symbol, the fatherhood of God, points the worshipper in the direction in which some important truths about God can be found. That is the intention of every symbol — to point to the thing being symbolised.

Some religions ban statues of any kind. They believe that it is blasphemous to try to represent God in any human form. Yet, as Hindus have realised, a statue is no more than a symbol of God. Hindus do not believe that such statues are gods. They simply use the statue as an aid to worship. It is a symbol which helps them to focus their hearts and minds on God.

Most religious buildings are full of symbols, from the altar-cross in a church [A], to the crescent in a mosque (C) and the seven-branched candlestick in a synagogue (B). Even the flag flying over a Sikh gurdwara is, in itself, a symbol. All of them remind the worshipper that God is over and beyond everything in life yet can be known by those who worship him.

A key question

Why are symbols so important in religious worship?

Do you know...

▶ what symbols help a religious worshipper to do?
▶ one very important Christian symbol which helps worshippers to understand God?
▶ a common Hindu symbol?

Things to do

1 **A** shows a very common Christian symbol.
   a What is the symbol?
   b Can you think of three ways in which this symbol has become part of our everyday lives?
   c What does it symbolise?

2 Christians, Jews, Muslims and Sikhs are strictly forbidden to make any statues representing God. For Christians and Jews the restriction is found in Exodus 20.4–6 as part of the Ten Commandments:

> 4"You shall not make for yourself an idol in the form of anything in heaven above or on the earth beneath or in the waters below. 5You shall not bow down to them or worship them; for I, the LORD your God, am a jealous God, punishing the children for the sin of the fathers to the third and fourth generation of those who hate me, 6but showing love to a thousand generations of those who love me and keep my commandments."

   a What reason does God give in this quotation for not allowing any idols or statues?
   b What are the two qualities demanded from those who would know the love of God?
   c Do you think that a statue could help people to worship God? Is there a danger here?

C What symbol can you see on top of this mosque?

Symbols in religion

7.2 Christian symbols

Christians have always found symbols to be useful. Sheltering from terrible persecution by the Roman Emperors, for example, the early Christians drew symbols on the walls of the catacombs beneath the city of Rome (**A**). This encouraged other Christians as they walked past to know that they were amongst friends. Their enemies, on the other hand, were unable to grasp the significance of the symbols. In other words, they became a kind of secret language. **A** shows one of the most popular symbols from this time — the sign of the fish. This symbol was used because each letter of the Greek word for 'fish' [icthus] stood for an important item of Christian belief:

A The sign of the fish was an early Christian symbol. What did it mean?

> I — Jesus
> C - Christ
> TH - God
> U - Son of
> S - Saviour

All that the early Christians believed was summed up in the single phrase 'Jesus Christ, Son of God, and Saviour'.

B

C

D

What is distinctive about each of the crosses shown in **B**, **C** and **D**?

As we discovered in Unit 5, Christian worship today is full of symbols. At the heart of the Eucharist, the most important Christian service of worship, stand the symbols of bread and wine. The Christian service of initiation, baptism, uses the symbol of water to speak of washing and new life. Through the serious and joyful festival of Easter with its many symbols Christians can enter into the meaning of the death and resurrection of Jesus. When a bishop lays his hands upon the heads of **confirmation** candidates Christians believe that they receive the same Holy Spirit whose coming is symbolised each year in the festival of **Whitsun.**

Yet the most important, and powerful, Christian symbol of all is the **cross.** As **B, C** and **D** show, no one is quite sure just what shape the cross should be but that does not matter. What matters is the truth which Christians believe is symbolised by the cross. This is that Jesus Christ, the Son of God, died for the sins of the world. So you will find crosses both inside and outside a church. Sometimes the figure of Christ appears on the cross (a **crucifix**). Christians often wear small crosses around their necks. Some Christians, mainly Roman Catholics, draw the sign of the cross on their bodies during certain acts of worship. The priest, at the end of the service, often blesses the congregation in the name of the Father, the Son and the Holy Spirit, making the sign of the cross as he does so.

A key question

What are the main symbols which play an important part in Christian worship?

Do you know...

▶ which symbol gave much courage to Christians suffering from Roman persecution?
▶ which Christian celebrations have great symbolic significance?
▶ which is the central Christian symbol?

Words to remember

Confirmation is the service at which Christians 'confirm' the vows which were made on their behalf at baptism.

The **cross** is the central symbol of the Christian faith, reminding believers of the death of Jesus of Nazareth.

The **crucifix** is a cross with the figure of Christ on it.

Whitsun is the Christian festival which celebrates the giving of the Holy Spirit on the first day of Pentecost.

Things to do

1 The following text was found on an early Christian tombstone. It suggests the thoughts of a man who was in danger of being persecuted:

> My name was Avircius, a disciple of the pure Shepherd, who feeds the flocks of sheep on mountains and plains, who has great and all-seeing eyes. He taught me the faithful Scriptures. To Rome he sent me. Everywhere I met with brethren. With Paul before me I followed, and Faith everywhere led the way and served food everywhere, the Fish from the spring — immense, pure, which the pure virgin caught and gave to her friends to eat for ever, with good wine, giving the cup with the wine.

The writer here uses many Christian symbols. How many can you find in this passage?

2 The cross, as **B, C** and **D** show, has taken many forms. See if you can find out from a library what was unusual about each of the following:

▶ Saint Anthony's Cross   ▶ Saint Andrew's Cross
▶ The Greek Orthodox Cross   ▶ The Maltese Cross
▶ The Cross of St George   ▶ The Celtic Cross

a Which organisation uses the Maltese Cross as its symbol today?
b Which cross are we most familiar with in this country?
c Design your own cross which would be suitable to use as a Christian symbol.

Symbols in religion

7.3 Jewish symbols

There are many symbols in the Jewish religion. One Jewish symbol is the **Star of David** [A]. Surprisingly, this was only chosen as a symbol of Judaism in the eighteenth century.

As Jews believe that it is possible to worship God equally well in the synagogue and in the home, so both of these places carry several symbols:

▶ whatever their size or location synagogues have certain symbolic features in common. Amongst the most important symbols found inside a synagogue are the Ark and the **everlasting light** which burns above it. You can see both of these clearly in **B.** The Ark is the holiest place in the synagogue since it houses the scrolls of God's teaching, the Torah.

▶ Jewish people think of the home itself as a symbol. Their religion provides guidelines for every aspect of life. Food is important to all of us and strict Jewish men and women follow a dietary code taken from the Jewish Scriptures. These laws (**kashrut**) are laid down in the Torah and the **Talmud.** They are symbols of the obedience and purity which God requires of Jews.

An important element in every Jewish home is the **mezuzah** (**C**). This is a small, hand-written scroll containing the **Shema.** The scroll is placed in a case and attached to the doorpost of the house. Some Jewish people touch the mezuzah with their finger-tips and lightly kiss them as they go in and

B What is kept in the Ark in a synagogue?

A Have you ever seen the Star of David? If not, keep your eyes open for it. If so, where did you see it?

C What is found inside the mezuzah and why might a Jew touch it as he or she goes in and comes out of a house?

come out of their house. In this way they are both showing respect for the Torah of which the Shema is an important part and being reminded to live a good life. The Shema, which is taken from Deuteronomy 6.4–9, says:

'Hear, O Israel; the Lord our God, the Lord is one. And you shall love the Lord your God with all your heart and with all your soul and with all your might.'

In such ways God's loving presence in both the synagogue and the Jewish home is recognised and symbolised. By acknowledging such symbols a Jew is announcing that he will be true to God and loving in his relationships with other members of the family and the community.

Words to remember

The **everlasting light** is the light above the Ark which reminds the Jew that God is always present with his people.

Kashrut are the Jewish dietary laws.

Biblical texts are inscribed on parchment and placed in a small container called the **mezuzah** and then fixed on the right-hand doorpost of a Jewish house.

The **Shema,** the Jewish statement of belief, takes its name from the first word of Deuteronomy 6.4.

The **Star of David** is a six-pointed star.

The **Talmud** is a book of commentaries and discussions based on the Torah.

A key question

What symbols which remind the Jew of God are to be found in the synagogue and in the home?

Do you know...

▶ what is symbolised by the light shining over the Ark?
▶ what the mezuzah is?
▶ what the Shema is?

Things to do

1   Copy this paragraph into your book and fill in the blanks from the words listed below:
The Jewish faith makes extensive use of _____, both in the _____ and in the _____. In the synagogue the _____ _____ above the _____ symbolises the _____ of God with his people. The _____ laws are a very important home symbol. These laws (the _____) are laid down in the _____ and the _____.

Torah   everlasting light   symbols   Talmud
synagogue   kashrut   home   presence
dietary   Ark

2   Below are four objects used in Jewish religious worship. Each of them symbolises something very important in the Jewish faith. Explain, in your own words, what each one is and what each one symbolises.
   a   The everlasting light
   b   The Holy Ark
   c   The kashrut
   d   The mezuzah

3   In a radio programme, 'Worlds of Faith', a Jewish mother explained how every act of her day became 'religious':

'All the daily chores of a woman become, for a Jewish woman, religious acts. For example, shopping, cleaning, cooking: when I go shopping I have to remember, and because of our dietary laws, I have to be very careful about the food I select in the market ... we elevate everything to God — even, for example, the cleaning; we have to clean before Shabbat (the Sabbath Day) and before the Holy Days (festivals) and that is actually a positive commandment.'

Why does this woman keep all these commandments? She went on to explain:

'Just because God commanded it ... There are many commandments we don't understand. We can try to find reasons for them but lots of them we don't understand.'

   a   What example does this woman give of turning the everyday things of life into religious acts?
   b   What reason does she give for doing this?

Symbols in religion

7.4 The symbols of Islam

The main symbols of Islam are the star and the **crescent moon** (A). Both of these are very important in the Middle East as they have been used to guide desert peoples for centuries. Muhammad grew up in a city in which both the stars and the moon were worshipped and he attacked this. At the same time they were suitable symbols for the new faith because Islam guides mankind (the star) and lights (the moon) the way of every believer through life.

As we have discovered, Muslims worship in a mosque. It is an important principle of Islam that, even though there is an Imam to lead the prayers, each person must come into God's presence to worship by himself. The shape of the building helps him to concentrate his mind on God. As **B** shows, the dome is an important feature of every mosque. This symbolises the heavens and the universe which Allah has created and over which he rules.

Although the number of minarets on a mosque varies there are usually four of them. The dome and the minarets together remind the Muslim of the Five Pillars of the Islam faith:

▶ the **Shahada** — the Muslim declaration of faith. You can find this in the blue box.
▶ the **Salat** — the obligation for regular prayer and worship.
▶ the **Zakat** — giving alms to the poor.
▶ the **Saum** — fasting during the month of Ramadan.
▶ the **Hajj** — a pilgrimage to the holy city of Makka.

A Which symbols can you see in this photograph and what do they mean?

B Why are the dome and the minaret important Muslim symbols?

C What does the act of prostration symbolise?

Muslims call the mosque a place of prostration. In the Qur'an Muhammad said:

> The whole earth has been made a place of prostration for me.

It is for this reason that Muslims can pray anywhere as long as they are in a 'clean place'. This, together with the washing rituals that must precede any prayer, are symbols of the purity that Allah requires from anyone who would worship him. A Muslim is someone who 'submits to the will of Allah'. The act of prostration during prayer (**C**) symbolises that submission and obedience.

Words to remember

The **crescent moon** is the waxing moon and so a suitable symbol of increasing power.

The **Hajj** is the pilgrimage to Makka which each Muslim is obliged to take once in his or her lifetime.

The **Shahada** is the Muslim declaration of faith.

The **Salat** is the obligation to pray five times a day.

The **Saum** is the practice of fasting, usually during the month of Ramadan.

The **Zakat** is the obligation on every Muslim to give 2½ per cent of his income each year to the poor.

A key question

What are the main symbols which play an important part in Islam?

Do you know...

▶ why the crescent moon and a star are suitable symbols for Islam?
▶ what the dome and the minarets in a mosque symbolise?
▶ what other symbols play an important part in Islam?

The Shahada

There is no god but God (Allah) and Muhammad is the Messenger of God.

▶ What are the two most important aspects of Muslim belief which are stressed in the Shahada?

Things to do

1 The Qur'an describes how Abraham (or Ibrahim) turned from worshipping the sun, moon and stars to the worship of Allah.

> Accordingly, We (God) showed Abraham the Kingdom of the heavens and of the earth, that he might be one of sure faith. As night darkened around him he beheld a star and said, 'This is my Lord'. But when it set, he said, 'I cannot love what sets'. And when he saw the moon rising he said, 'If my Lord does not guide me aright, I shall surely be among the erring'. And when he saw the sun rising he said, 'This is my Lord, this is greater'. But when it also set he said, 'O my people, I have finished with all your idolatrous things. As for me my face is towards the One who created the heaven and the earth, as a man of pure faith. I am not a worshipper of false deities.'

a Why do you think that Abraham, who lived in a desert area, was tempted to worship the stars, moon and sun?
b What was it that persuaded him not to worship them in the end?
c What was there about God which made him greater than the heaven and the earth?
d Which phrase did Abraham apply to the stars, moon and sun?

2 A Muslim must wash himself before praying and prostrate himself as he prays. Explain in your own words why these actions are important and what they mean.

Symbols in religion

7.5 The statue as a symbol of God

Every Hindu has his or her own understanding of God which they use as a way of knowing the one God, **Brahman.** Every physical object in the universe is thought to be part of God. Because of this anything can be used as a focus for worship as long as the worshipper remembers that it is only a means of worshipping God and not God itself. Eventually every Hindu hopes, through many rebirths, to achieve union with Brahman. His or her life on earth will then be over. Meanwhile every statue of God is a means to help the soul on its upward march and bring that moment of union closer.

Each individual finds his or her own god full of symbolism. We can see this if we look at one of the most popular statues in Hinduism, that of

Ganesha, the god with the head of an elephant (**A**). Notice:

▶ that Ganesha has four hands. In two hands he holds a rosary and a goad (stick). The rosary symbolises Ganesha's control over death whilst the goad is used to regulate the way that each person behaves. In his two other hands are an axe by which he destroys ignorance and sweets to reward those whose ignorance has been destroyed.

▶ that around Ganesha's neck there is a snake, the symbol of death, which the god controls.

▶ that being an elephant but sitting on a mouse shows Ganesha's concern for all, great and small.

A There is a Hindu legend to explain why Ganesha was given the head of an elephant. Can you find out what it is?

B Krishna holding up Mount Govardhana. Who is Krishna?

▶ that from Ganesha's mouth comes the sacred sound Aum. According to the Hindu Scriptures this is God's name and so must be said regularly by all Hindu believers. Made up of three basic letters of the alphabet, the sound shows that God is at the heart of life itself.

Words to remember

When a Hindu speaks of **Brahman** he means the holy power beyond the universe. Brahman cannot be described and can only be spoken of as 'Not this; Not that'.

Ganesha is popular in Hinduism as the god of wisdom and good fortune.

A key question

How does a Hindu use statues in order to worship God?

C Who, or what, is being worshipped by this Hindu?

Do you know...

▶ whether Hindus believe in thousands of different gods or one God?
▶ what a Hindu eventually hopes to achieve?
▶ what symbols are found on a statue of the popular god with the head of an elephant, Ganesha?

Things to do

1 Fit together the phrases below to make a sensible paragraph. Make a rough draft and see if your friends agree. Then copy it out neatly.
   a to help the people draw nearer to Brahman;
   b although there are many gods in Hinduism;
   c in its upward march to God;
   d they are all representations of the one God, Brahman.
   e each god is an aid;
   f each statue of a god is a symbol;
   g to achieve union with Brahman;
   h to help the soul.

2 In **B** the god Krishna is lifting up Mount Govardhana to protect the herdsmen and their cows from rain brought on by Indra, the weather and war god. Study the picture carefully before going on to answer these questions:
   a Indra was an early Hindu god of war, rain and thunder. He was not at all pleased by the challenge that Krishna made to his authority. How can we see this displeasure symbolised in the picture?
   b Krishna is one of the most popular of the Hindu gods today. He is believed to have considerable power and authority. Can you see how this is symbolised in the picture?
   c When he was on earth, Krishna was recognised by many to be a god. Are there any symbols in this picture to show that Krishna was recognised to be a god by those around him?
   d If Hindus believe that each of their many gods represents a different aspect of Brahman's character then what would be the value of preserving a story which shows two gods quarrelling with each other?

7.6 The Sikh faith and its symbols

Although Sikhism is a religious faith it is much more than that. It is a community of believers, a fellowship and a brotherhood. Although a Sikh can offer prayer to God at any time there must be regular occasions when Sikhs meet with their fellow believers to worship God (**A**). As the Guru Granth Sahib says:

> The highest and most beneficial deed is the Lord's praise in the holy congregation.

The gurdwara, the place of worship, is a symbol of that spiritual unity which exists amongst all Sikhs and is such a feature of their faith. The flag which flies above every gurdwara is both a symbol of that unity and an announcement to the community that here is a Sikh place of worship. Indeed the flag itself contains several symbols (**C**). The Sikh flag is triangular and has a **khanda** on a yellow background. The khanda is made up of:

▶ two **kirpans** or swords
▶ a chakar or circle
▶ the khanda

As you can see, the central symbols of the flag are military. This is because each Sikh sees himself as being a warrior saint. In times past he has often been called upon to defend his faith by taking up the sword. This military aspect is further emphasised by the fact that another khanda is placed at the head of the flag-pole. The Sikh emblem on the flag is normally blue.

A Sikh's life is governed by his adherence to the Five Ks — kesh, kanga, kara, kachs and kirpan. These carry a particular symbolic significance for every Sikh. You found out about that in Book One. Elsewhere in this book [Unit 2.5] we also looked at the Sikh holy book – the Guru Granth Sahib – and underlined the great reverence with which it is treated. Sikhs do not, however, worship the book. Worship belongs to God alone. The Guru Granth Sahib is reverenced so highly because of what it symbolises. Whenever it is present a building becomes a gurdwara and so God is known to be there.

A Write down three features of Sikh worship that you can detect from this photograph.

B Where is the Sikh flag erected?

C What are the three parts of the emblem on the Sikh flag?

Words to remember

A **khanda** is a double-edged sword which represents both power and divinity.

A **kirpan** is a short sword carried by members of the Sikh community as a symbol of their active resistance to evil.

A key question

Which symbols are most important in Sikh worship?

Do you know...

▶ what the flag flying above a gurdwara symbolises?
▶ what the symbols to be seen on the Sikh flag are?
▶ why the Five Ks and the Guru Granth Sahib are very important because of what they symbolise?

Things to do

1 The Guru Granth Sahib says this about the gurdwara:

> Holy congregation is the school of the True Guru. There we learn to love God and appreciate his goodness.

The gurdwara is a symbol of that unity which binds Sikh to Sikh but:
  a Who do you think that the 'True Guru' is, and why is he called 'True'?
  b What is a congregation?
  c Why is it called 'holy'?
  d Why is the holy congregation called the 'school' of the True Guru?
  e In learning to appreciate their unity with each other what two things does a Sikh learn about God?

2 In **B** you can see a Sikh flag being erected during the Baisakhi (New Year) ceremony.
  a What do all flags have in common with each other? In other words, what do flags symbolise?
  b There are three distinct symbols shown on the Sikh flag. What are they? What do they symbolise collectively?
  c Why do you think that a flag is chosen to let everyone know that a particular building is a gurdwara?
  d Design a flag for one of the following religions using appropriate symbols drawn from that particular religion:

  Christianity   Judaism   Islam

Unit 8 Travelling

8.1 Visiting the holy places

A **pilgrimage** is a journey undertaken by followers of a religion to places which are considered particularly holy. Some people undertake such a journey for the sense of peace that it can bring. Others use a pilgrimage to express the deep feelings that they have about God. Some religions place a solemn obligation upon their devotees to undertake a pilgrimage. Other religions leave people free to undertake a pilgrimage if they want to.

There are many holy places in Hinduism and Hindus are likely to make many visits during their lifetime. Often the main reason for their journey is to meet their guru [spiritual teacher] who lives at the site [**A**]. Although such holy places can be in the mountains or elsewhere, Hindus have long regarded the rivers of India as being the most holy places of all. This is particularly true of any place where, as at **Banaras,** two rivers meet.

When the Jewish Temple was still standing in Jerusalem 2000 years ago all Jews were expected to travel to the city for the three pilgrimage feasts each year. The Temple has long since gone but thousands of pilgrims still make a pilgrimage to the holy city. The same city is also sacred to Christians and Muslims. The city which the Sikhs regard as their spiritual home is Amritsar, and they often make a pilgrimage there.

Although Christians are not obliged to make a pilgrimage, thousands do visit the Holy Land and other places associated with Jesus. Some Christians also travel to places such as Lourdes in France and Walsingham in Norfolk, where the Virgin Mary is said to have appeared.

A Hindu pilgrims meet their guru. What is a guru?

B These pilgrims at Lourdes are taking away bottles of water. What special properties do you think this water is believed to have?

No one is under a stronger obligation to make a pilgrimage than a Muslim. As long as they are fit and healthy Muslims must make the Hajj to **Makka** once in their lifetime. On the pilgrimage they are also likely to visit other places which have played an important part in their religious history. You can find out more about the Hajj in Unit 8.5.

C Which city are all healthy Muslims obliged to visit?

Words to remember

Situated on the banks of the River Ganges, **Banaras** is one of the most sacred places for all Hindus. To die in Banaras is regarded as a great happiness as it is considered to be the gateway to the after-life.

Makka, the birthplace of Muhammad and the spiritual home of Islam, is situated in modern Saudi Arabia.

A **pilgrimage** is any journey undertaken for a religious motive.

A key question

Why have people always gone on religious pilgrimages?

Do you know...

▶ which are the holiest places of all for Hindus?
▶ which city is holy to three different religions?
▶ who makes a special journey to Makka and what that journey is called?

Things to do

1   Five words connected with visiting sacred places are hidden in this word puzzle (the words read either across or down). Find the words and explain what they mean.

L	A	M	E	C	T	C	A	G	N
B	A	N	A	R	A	S	D	O	L
T	F	K	I	V	M	W	I	R	H
E	M	L	J	G	P	R	J	G	U
M	L	W	Q	S	L	U	V	H	D
P	A	G	J	M	A	K	K	A	J
L	O	U	R	D	E	S	S	J	T
E	O	J	N	Z	R	C	V	J	I
P	A	M	E	D	Z	V	U	S	T

2   In the Qur'an all Muslims are commanded to undertake a pilgrimage to Makka at some time. Here are the words:

> Exhort all men to make the pilgrimage. They will come on foot, and on the backs of swift camels and from every distant quarter. Let the pilgrims spruce themselves, make their vows and circle the Ancient House.
> Such is Allah's commandment. He that reveres the sacred rites of Allah shall fare better in the sight of the Lord.

a   Why do you think that some religions lay a heavy obligation upon a believer to make a pilgrimage whilst others do not?

b   What do you think that a religious worshipper might gain from making a pilgrimage to a holy place?

c   Do you have a secret hiding place? A favourite holiday spot? A friend or a relative who means a lot to you? If so, describe the place or person and try to explain just why they are so special.

8.2 The city of Jerusalem

Jerusalem is a holy city for Jews, Christians and Muslims alike. It was here, long ago, that King David built his capital city and where his son, Solomon, put up the first great Temple. After this Temple was destroyed one attempt was made to rebuild, around 538 BCE. Then, just before Jesus was born, King Herod began to build another Temple, but within years of being completed it was pulled down and burnt by the Romans. No further attempt was made to rebuild.

All that now remains of Herod's majestic building in the city is the **Western Wall.** For hundreds of years Jewish pilgrims have prayed at the foot of this wall, rocking backwards and forwards reciting their holy Torah [**A**]. In this way they are expressing their great sorrow that the Jewish nation has been dispersed throughout the world. They are also praying for God's future blessing upon Jews everywhere. These strong feelings keep Jerusalem at the centre of the Jewish faith.

Christians, of course, associate Jerusalem with the life of Jesus Christ. As a Jew, anticipating death, he made his way to the city of Jerusalem because he considered it to be the only appropriate place for a Jewish prophet to die. In the courtyard of the Roman governor he was tried and sentenced to death. In the same city, three days later, his disciples celebrated the return of Jesus from the dead. To celebrate these events thousands of Christian pilgrims congregate in Jerusalem each year at Easter time and visit the **Church of the Holy Sepulchre** [B].

After Makka Jerusalem is the most important, and sacred, city in Muslim history. Muslims also have their own shrine in the city, **The Dome of the Rock,** which commemorates the 'Night Journey' which the Prophet Muhammad is believed to have made on a winged horse led by the Archangel Gabriel to the Temple at Jerusalem. It was here that he met with Abraham, Moses and Jesus before ascending through the seven spheres (areas) of Heaven into the presence of Allah. From Allah's presence Muhammad returned to earth to preach the message that he had received. It was this message that persuaded many people to become Muslims.

A What are these Jews doing at the Western Wall?

Words to remember

The Church of the Holy Sepulchre in Jerusalem is built on the supposed site of the tomb of Jesus.

The Dome of the Rock is the Islamic shrine built in Jerusalem. It is a mosque.

Jerusalem is the capital of modern Israel but also contains the Church of the Holy Sepulchre (**B**) and the Dome of the Rock.

The **Western Wall** is the only part of Herod's Temple still standing, and a place of pilgrimage for Jews.

A key question

What is there in Jerusalem to indicate that the city is sacred to three different religions?

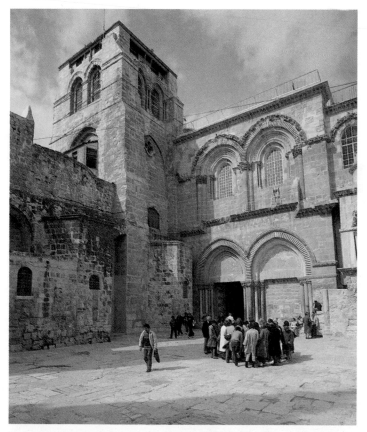

B On the site of what is the Church of the Holy Sepulchre believed to have been built?

Do you know...

▶ what makes the city of Jerusalem sacred to Jews, Christians and Muslims?
▶ what the Western Wall is?
▶ what the Church of the Holy Sepulchre is?
▶ what the Dome of the Rock is?

Things to do

1 Answer each of these questions in a complete sentence and in your own words:
   a Which religions look upon the city of Jerusalem as being particularly sacred?
   b Who established his capital in the old city of Jerusalem?
   c Which king built the first Temple in Jerusalem?
   d What now remains in Jerusalem of King Herod's Temple?
   e Which Christian festival draws thousands of pilgrims to Jerusalem?
   f What is the name of the mosque that Muslims have built in Jerusalem?

2 On one occasion St Matthew tells us that Jesus was very upset over the future of the city of Jerusalem. He records Jesus as saying:

> [37]"O Jerusalem, Jerusalem, you who kill the prophets and stone those sent to you, how often I have longed to gather your children together, as a hen gathers her chicks under her wings, but you were not willing. [38]Look, your house is left to you desolate."
>
> Matthew 23.37–8

   a What did Jesus mean when he said that he had often wanted to gather Jerusalem's children together?
   b When was the Temple in Jerusalem left standing 'desolate'?

3 Visit your nearest library and find out as much as you can about the Church of the Holy Sepulchre and the Dome of the Rock. Write the information into your book as a project. Try to find pictures of these two religious buildings and then explain why they are so important to Christians and Muslims.

8.3 Christian holy places

As we saw earlier, a pilgrimage is a journey to a place which is, for some reason, considered to be holy. For Christians this has meant two things:

▶ visiting those places in the Holy Land where events in the life of Jesus occurred.
▶ visiting those places in which saints are thought to have had visions or are buried.

The holy places in this country which have been visited by pilgrims have all been associated with saints. The pilgrims who have travelled to them for centuries have had many reasons for going — to give thanks for something that the saint is thought to have done, to say a special prayer, to seek healing or to perform an act of repentance.

B Which group of Christians visit Rome to receive a blessing from the Pope?

A Why did pilgrims begin to visit Lourdes in France?

In Europe there are many places which Christian pilgrims have travelled to in the past, and still do today. With its many associations with the early Christian Church, Rome has long been a popular destination for pilgrims. During festival times pilgrims gather in St Peter's Square to receive the Pope's blessing. Pilgrims in Italy also go to Assisi, the home of St Francis. It was in 1986 that the Archbishop of Canterbury, the Pope and other Church leaders met in Assisi to pray for the peace of the world.

Often people undertake a pilgrimage seeking healing. It was at **Lourdes,** in 1858, that a 14-year-old girl, Bernadette, had a series of visions. A spring of water appeared and then a series of miraculous healings is thought to have started. Millions of pilgrims have visited Lourdes and even though a very small handful appear to have been cured others have found a sense of peace.

A similar shrine to that in Lourdes can be found in England at **Walsingham** in Norfolk. A well in this small village is thought to have similar healing properties to the one in Lourdes. The shrine at Walsingham was destroyed in the sixteenth century during the Reformation but it was rebuilt in the early part of this century. Anglicans and Catholics now visit the shrine and process through the village each year.

Words to remember

A series of miraculous healings from 1873 onwards has brought thousands of pilgrims to the French village of **Lourdes.**

Lady Recheldis had a vision in the eleventh century of the Virgin Mary in which she was told to build an exact copy of the house of Jesus in Nazareth. This she did in **Walsingham** in Norfolk.

A key question

Where are the main Christian shrines and why do people still make pilgrimages to them?

Do you know...

▶ why Christian pilgrims might decide to visit a holy shrine?
▶ why many Christians might make a pilgrimage to Rome?
▶ what the link is between the Christian shrines at Lourdes and Walsingham?

Things to do

1 Here are five definitions. Your task is to decide which words are being defined:
   a The Christian shrine founded as the result of a vision given to a 14-year-old girl.
   b The centre of pilgrimage which was the home of a saint who became famous for his care of animals and birds.
   c The country in which Jesus lived and which has many places of Christian pilgrimage.
   d The square in which Christians gather to receive a blessing from the Pope.
   e The shrine which is based upon the house in which Jesus grew up in Nazareth.

2 Copy an outline map of Europe into your book. Using this unit, and your own research, put as many places of Christian pilgrimage as you can on your map.
   To help you: As well as those mentioned in this unit, the following are also important centres of pilgrimage: Canterbury, Santiago de Compostello in Spain, Lindisfarne, Iona, and Knock in Ireland.

   Can you discover what is thought to have happened at ONE of these centres of pilgrimage?

3 Try to find someone who has undertaken a pilgrimage as a Christian and invite them to answer your questions:
   ▶ Where did they go?
   ▶ What did they expect to gain from the pilgrimage?
   ▶ How difficult did they find the pilgrimage?
   ▶ Did they meet other Christians on the pilgrimage and did this add to their enjoyment?
   ▶ What did they think they had gained from the pilgrimage once it was over?
   ▶ Would they undertake a pilgrimage again?

8.4 Coventry Cathedral

On one terrible night in November 1940 German bombers dropped bomb after bomb on the city of Coventry. Many of the bombs fell on the Cathedral Church of St Michael. You can see from photograph **A** the awful devastation that this caused. Although, at the time, many people said that the work of rebuilding the church would begin immediately, it was not until 1951 that the work of reconstruction began.

After giving the matter serious thought the architect, Basil Spence, decided to use the remains of the old building as the entrance to the new Cathedral. A wooden cross, made from the charred roof timbers, was then placed upon the old altar which was still in place (**B**). This altar and wooden cross now provide a focal point for the many open-air services that are held in the Cathedral precincts. If you look carefully at **B** you will also find, behind the altar, the words 'Father, forgive' carved in the wall.

Ever since the new building was opened in 1962 it has become a place of pilgrimage for many Christians from all over the world. This is partly due to the peace and the beauty of the new building but it is more than that. Pilgrims are also drawn by what the new Cathedral stands for and symbolises:

▶ The bombing of the old building has been taken as a symbol of the foolishness and waste of war. This message is made very clear to all who visit the building by the remains of the old building which are to be seen everywhere.

▶ Christians feel the confidence in the resurrection and hope which are at the heart of the faith when the 'phoenix' of the new Cathedral is able to rise from the 'ashes' of the old. Just as Jesus rose from the death of despair so a new monument to God rose out of the inhumanity of war.

A The ruins of the old Coventry Cathedral after the German bombing. What kind of impact do you think this might have had on the neighbourhood?

HOLY, HOLY, HOLY, LORD GOD OF HOSTS HEAVEN AND EARTH ARE FULL OF THY GLORY

B Do you think that some people might have been upset to see the words 'Father, forgive' carved on the wall of the new Cathedral? If so, why?

Even the reclaiming of the land, following the end of the Second World War, was a parable in itself. The cry went up from Coventry for help to rebuild the Cathedral of St Michael. Christians and non-Christians from across the world responded willingly. Amongst those who offered their voluntary help were many young people from Germany.

A key question

Why has Coventry Cathedral become a symbol of the Christian faith which draws pilgrims from across the world?

C Do you think that the new Coventry Cathedral looks very different from the old building?

Do you know...

▶ how Coventry Cathedral was destroyed and by whom?
▶ how the ruins of the old Cathedral were treated when the new building was erected and why?
▶ what the new building at Coventry symbolises to the many pilgrims who visit it each year?

Things to do

1 As you approach the front of Coventry Cathedral the first thing that you see is a large statue by Jacob Epstein. It shows the Archangel Michael standing with his foot firmly placed upon the devil. You can see it in **D**.
   a Describe all that you can see in the photograph.
   b Why do you think that a statue showing the Archangel Michael with his foot upon the devil is particularly appropriate for the outside of Coventry Cathedral? In what way might Christians claim that the rebuilding of the Cathedral represents the defeat of the devil?

2 Imagine that you were a regular worshipper in the Cathedral Church of St Michael, Coventry. You walk past on the morning after an air raid and you find the church in ruins. **A** will help you to imagine what the scene was like.
   a Describe how you might have felt on that morning.
   b Describe how you might have felt when the new Cathedral was opened and you were able to worship in the Cathedral once more.

3 Find out as much as you can about the old building of St Michael and the new Cathedral which has grown up on the same spot. Try to discover why so many pilgrims have found the new Cathedral to be such a strong and powerful symbol of new life and hope.

D Who has conquered whom in this sculpture?

8.5 The pilgrimage to Makka

All healthy adult Muslims, male and female, are under an obligation to make the Hajj, the pilgrimage to the holy city of Makka, once during their lifetime. It is one of the Five Pillars of the faith. As the Qur'an tells them:

> Make the pilgrimage and visit the Sacred House for His sake . . . Make the pilgrimage in the appointed month.

The 'appointed month' is the twelfth in the Muslim calendar. Each year between one and two million pilgrims make their pilgrimage to Makka from all corners of the earth using all possible means of transport. **A** shows just a small part of one pilgrim group en route.

As the pilgrims reach the outskirts of Makka they put on two pieces of cloth [**Ihram**] and call out: 'We have come in answer to your call, O Lord'. Once in the city each pilgrim performs the **Tawaf** by walking seven times (three times quickly and four times slowly) around the **Ka'ba.** You can see this cube-like shrine in **B.** Then, moving in an anti-clockwise direction and keeping the Ka'ba on their left-hand side, each pilgrim tries to kiss the **Black Stone** at the base of the Ka'ba. This stone was believed to have been given by God to Abraham and was once white but has now turned black because of mankind's wrong-doing.

You can see from map **C** the journey that the pilgrims take once they have left Makka. It was between the hills of Safa and Marwa that Ishmail's mother ran frantically to and fro seeking water — only to discover that her young son had been shown a well in the desert by God anyway. To relive this event each pilgrim must run the 366 metres between the two hills seven times.

On the next day, after sunrise, the pilgrims set out for Mount Arafat. Some walk and others ride. Once there the pilgrims offer prayers remembering the words of Muhammad that '. . . the best of prayers is that of the day of Arafat'. Then, after spending a night in the open, the pilgrims collect 49 stones on their way to Mina. Once there they throw the stones at three concrete pillars. These pillars represent the Shaitan (devil) and remind the pilgrim that Ishmail was tempted to rebel against his father, Abraham. It is believed that Abraham drove the Shaitan away by throwing stones at him and it is this that the pilgrim imitates.

The great festival of **Eid-Ul-Adha** is then celebrated by all Muslims whether they are on the pilgrimage or not. Just as Abraham offered up a sacrifice of a sheep instead of his son, so all Muslims are expected to offer a similar sacrifice. In this way Muslims everywhere are sharing in the blessings that all those who have participated in the pilgrimage have enjoyed.

A A pilgrim camp near Makka. What do you think that the pilgrims get from living together like this on their pilgrimage?

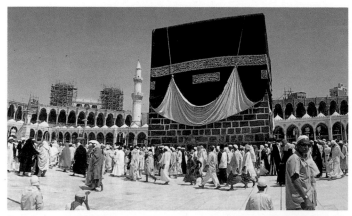

B Can you find out why pilgrims walk seven times around the Ka'ba?

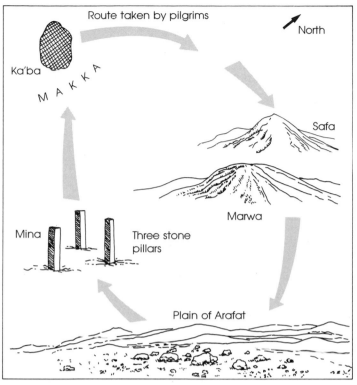

C What happens between Safa and Marwa and at Mina?

Words to remember

One of the most sacred objects in Islam, the **Black Stone,** is set in the south-east corner of the Ka'ba.

The **Eid-Ul-Adha** is the Festival of Sacrifice which takes place when pilgrims reach Mina.

Ihram are the two cotton cloths that a pilgrim must put on before entering Makka. One of them is wound around the waist and the other is draped across the left shoulder. Women cover the head and the rest of the body with Ihram.

The **Ka'ba** is the sacred shrine in Makka, set in the courtyard of the Mosque, towards which all Muslims turn when they pray.

Tawaf involves walking around the Ka'ba seven times as part of the pilgrimage to Makka.

A key question

Why do pilgrims journey to Makka and what do they do on the journey?

Do you know...

▶ what pilgrims shout out when they reach the outskirts of Makka?
▶ what pilgrims do in the city of Makka?
▶ what pilgrims do after they leave Makka?

Things to do

1 Muslim pilgrims wear Ihram on the outskirts of Makka.
   a What is Ihram?
   b Why do you think that every pilgrim has to wear exactly the same clothes?

2 A booklet issued by the Muslim Educational Trust says this about the Hajj:

> Hajj symbolises the unity of mankind ... Hajj stands as the peak of the obligatory duties in that it lays bare to a Muslim that he belongs to none other than his Creator. Hajj also demonstrates the equality of mankind.

   a How does the practice of wearing identical clothes tie in with this quotation?
   b What three reasons are given to explain why the pilgrimage to Makka means so much to a Muslim?

3 Here are two Muslims speaking after their experience of making a pilgrimage to Makka.

> 'It is every Muslim's ambition to visit the blessed clty Makka and kiss the Black Stone. For me that was a very beautiful experience. It was also very moving to visit the Prophet Muhammad's tomb.'

> 'Although it is many years since I went on the Hajj I can still remember very clearly how I felt when I stood in front of the Ka'ba. Once you are there you feel that you are in paradise and not on earth at all. The actual journey may be hard work but once you are there everything is so worthwhile.'

   a What do you think there was about standing in front of the Prophet Muhammad's tomb that made it such a moving experience for the first speaker?
   b What could the second speaker mean when he spoke about his visit to Makka as feeling like being in paradise?

8.6 The City of Banaras

Rivers play a very important part in the everyday lives of the people of India. As they alone can provide the fertility that the surrounding country-side needs, as well as water for washing, drinking and cooking, they are looked upon as 'mother goddesses'. Most of the holy places in India to which pilgrims travel regularly are situated on the banks of rivers.

The most popular of all the holy places is the city of **Banaras** [A]. Its sacred nature derives from its geographical location — on the banks of the River Ganga at the point where the river meets its smaller tributary, the Varuna. The meeting-place of two rivers is thought to be particularly holy. Its status amongst Hindus is greatly enhanced by the belief that it was here that the great god **Shiva** lived. This draws more than a million pilgrims to the city each year, and when they arrive they discover that there are more than a thousand temples in this one city alone dedicated to Shiva.

Shiva [**B**] is the Hindu god of life, death and rebirth. He is the visible expression of that force which both creates and destroys life. As you can see from **B**, he is often shown performing the Tandava, or world-shattering dance. Hindus are not too sure what to make of Shiva and they appear to love him and fear him in equal measure.

Along the three-mile stretch of the Ganga in Banaras there are steps (**ghats**) from which Hindu pilgrims are able to bathe in the holy waters of the river. This cleans the body after a long journey but also, more importantly, cleanses the soul from all evil. 'Burning ghats' are the steps on which cremations are carried out before the ashes and sacred marigold flowers are placed in the waters. It is the dearest wish of every Hindu to die in Banaras and to have his or her ashes scattered on the waters of the Ganga. This will guarantee that the soul will pass straight to Brahman without needing to be reborn again.

A What takes place on these ghats on the banks of the Ganga?

B Why is the god Shiva both loved and feared by many Hindus?

Words to remember

One of the most holy cities in India, **Banaras,** is situated on the banks of the River Ganga.

Ghats are steps or platforms at the edges of holy rivers from which people bathe and on which cremations take place.

Shiva, the 'mild one', is one of the greatest of the Hindu gods. In statues Shiva is sometimes shown performing the Tandava, a world-shattering dance.

Do you know...

▶ where the city of Banaras is situated and what makes its position so important?
▶ which god is worshipped at Banaras in particular?
▶ what the Hindu pilgrim does when he reaches Banaras?

A key question

Why is the city of Banaras particularly important to all Hindus?

Things to do

1 Copy and complete these sentences:
   a _____ play a very important part in the lives of the Indian people.
   b The rivers are looked upon as _____ by the Indian people.
   c _____ is the most popular Hindu sacred place because it is believed to be the place where the god _____ lived.
   d Of the seven holy rivers in India the most important is the _____.
   e Banaras is situated at the point where the River _____ and the River _____ meet. This makes it particularly _____ for Hindus.

2 In your own words, write a short description of Banaras. Try to explain just why it is such an important place for Hindu pilgrims.

3 **A** shows the many ghats along the bank of the River Ganga. Explain what a visitor to the city might expect to find taking place on these ghats as he or she walks along the river bank.

4 Eric Newby is a traveller who has written many books. In *Slowly down the Ganges* he writes about the holy river:

   It is great because, to millions of Hindus it is the most sacred, venerated river on earth. To bathe in it is to wash away guilt. To drink the water, having bathed in it, and to carry away bottles for those who have not had the great fortune to make the pilgrimage is meritorious. To be cremated on its banks, having died there, is the wish of every Hindu. Even to ejaculate 'Ganga, Ganga', at the distance of fifty-five kilometres from the river may atone for the sins committed during three previous lives.

   a What do Hindus believe happens to anyone who bathes in the waters of the river?
   b What two hopes make up the wish of every Hindu?

8.7 The Golden Temple at Amritsar

A Who built the Golden Temple at Amritsar and when?

The Guru Granth Sahib tells all Sikhs:

> If a man goes to bathe at a place of pilgrimage with the mind of a crook and the body of a thief, his exterior will be washed by bathing, of course, but his inside will be twice as unclean. He will be like the gourd, clean on the outside but full of poison within.

What matters, therefore, is the spiritual state in which each Sikh undertakes a pilgrimage. The pilgrimage will only draw him closer to God if he is prepared to give up his evil ways. If so, he may join thousands of other pilgrims travelling to the **Golden Temple** at **Amritsar** confident that he will receive a blessing from God.

The city of Amritsar was founded by Guru Ram Das so that Sikhs could come and worship God. Those working on the city dug out a lake which

B The Guru-Ka-Langar, the communal kitchen at the Golden Temple. How did Guru Arjan encourage people of any faith, caste or rank to sit down and take food together?

was called Amrit Sarowar ('a Pool of Nectar'). Guru Arjan then built the Golden Temple in the middle (**A**). Holding a special place in the affections of all Sikhs, the Golden Temple is believed to be the 'Court of the Lord'. Gold leaf covers the outside of the building whilst inside the walls are covered with beautiful paintings. Over the Dehri (gateway to the temple) is located a treasury in which there used to be four sets of golden doors, jewelled canopies and umbrellas, together with the golden spades which were used to inaugurate the desilting of the lake in 1923. All these articles were destroyed during the invasion of the Golden Temple complex by the Indian army in 1984.

One very important feature of the Golden Temple is that holy hymns are sung there non-stop day and night. It upset Sikhs throughout the world, therefore, when, in 1984, the Indian army invaded the Temple. They were trying to remove Sikh militants who had been using the Temple as a fortress. The building itself hardly suffered any damage but many people lost their lives.

Words to remember

Amritsar is the sacred city of the Sikhs in the Punjab, founded by the fourth Guru.

The **Golden Temple** is the centre of Sikh pilgrimage and was built by the fifth Guru, Arjan, beside the Pool of Immortality.

A key question

Why is the Golden Temple at Amritsar such an important place of Sikh pilgrimage?

Do you know...

▶ what the Guru Granth Sahib has to say about the dangers of pilgrimages?
▶ why the location of the Golden Temple is spiritually significant?
▶ what upset Sikhs throughout the world in 1984?

Things to do

1 Here are some answers to a crossword. Write down what you think the clues might have been.

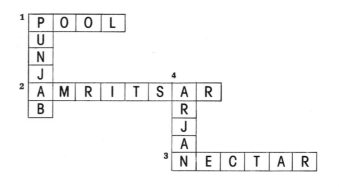

2 When asked on one occasion 'Should I go and bathe at a pilgrimage place?' Guru Nanak replied 'God's Name is the real pilgrimage place'. As the quotation from the Guru Granth Sahib on the opposite page suggests, the Sikh gurus were really against pilgrimages.
   a What is the main reason given for this?
   b Why should the crook and the thief be twice as unclean after a pilgrimage as they were before going on one?
   c What do you think that Guru Nanak meant when he said that 'God's Name is the real pilgrimage place'?
   d If a person is prepared to give up their evil ways before a pilgrimage, what benefit might the holy journey have?

3 In the days of Guru Arjan there were two main religions in India, Hinduism and Islam. Neither would allow members of the other faith to enter their religious buildings. Guru Arjan was very unhappy about this and said:

   God gives air, water and sunshine to everybody, so all have equal rights to thank God for his gifts and sings his praises. So temples should be open to all.

   a What was Guru Arjan's main reason for insisting that religious buildings should be open for everyone to worship God?
   b Do you agree with Guru Arjan that temples (or any place of worship) should be open to all? Explain your answer.

Words to remember — unit references